HATS & BELLS
Children's Party Cookbook

HATTY STEAD AND ANNABEL WALEY-COHEN

PHOTOGRAPHY BY JEMMA WATTS

KYLE BOOKS

To our parents – George & Daffy Stead and
Bertie & Serena Ballin... Thank you for all the memories!

**First published in Great Britain in 2013 by
Kyle Books
an imprint of Kyle Cathie Limited
67–69 Whitfield Street
London W1T 4HF
general.enquiries@kylebooks.com
www.kylebooks.com**

ISBN: 978 0 85783 177 4

A CIP catalogue record for this title is available from
the British Library.

Text © Hatty Stead and Annabel Waley-Cohen 2013
Photographs © Jemma Watts 2013
Design © Kyle Books 2013

Editor: Vicky Orchard
Design: Lucy Parissi
Photography: Jemma Watts
Food styling: Gee Charman
Prop styling: Pippa Jameson
Copy editor: Nikki Sims
Proofreader: Jane Bamforth
Production: Nic Jones and David Hearn

Colour reproduction by ALTA London
Printed and bound in China by C & C Offset Printing Co., Ltd.

Contents

Foreword   4

Let's Throw a Party!   6

Cakes   16

Teddy Bears' Picnic   18

Farmyard Fun   38

Wizards and Fairies   58

Knights and Princesses   74

Under the Sea   92

Space and Star Odyssey   110

Circus, Circus   128

Wild, Wild West   148

Ghosts, Ghouls and Goblins   168

Last-Minute Panic Party   188

Directory   204

Index   206

Foreword

sk anyone to recall a memory from their childhood and the chances are they will start pondering over a birthday party they once had or at least went to. Whether it be a taste, a smell or something more visual, celebrations evoke strong memories in all our minds, no matter how many moons ago they were. When interviewed by the *Party Times*, we were asked about our childhood birthdays and it was interesting to see that we had such vivid recollections, from not just our own parties but from siblings' and friends' too.

Annabel can remember her favourite blue and white smocked dress, which she refused to ever take off; a chocolate buttercream cake topped with sugary white icing, wrapped tentatively in a napkin; typical 1980s party bags, filled with pink sugar mice, psychedelic yoyos and those red fortune-telling fish, which curled up in your hand and breaking down in tears when someone gave her a paper case filled with a curdled mess of jelly and rapidly melting ice cream (she still, to this day, cannot eat clear and cloudy food together!) Perhaps the grandest moment of all, was when Mrs Tiggywinkle appeared over the hilltops with a layered, pocketed skirt, which was filled with little presents for each guest.

With a birthday falling in May, Hatty's childhood memories are filled with wonderful images of playing in the spring sunshine with friends and family before gathering around a picnic blanket for her birthday tea. Her mother used to create the most wonderful treats; she still remembers standing on a chair, covered in flour, peering over the kitchen surface, watching her create cupcakes, cookies and colourful meringues. Once the party day arrived, she swapped a flour-stained top for a favourite party dress and would be pacing the hallway, hardly able to contain her excitement, before that first friend arrived. She had so many birthday antics over the years, from performing plays and dressing up as a princess, to games of rounders with her whole class, followed by a beautiful homemade birthday tea.

The parties that we enjoyed were always imaginative and engaging, with delicious food to match. Reading back through this, one realises how simple these memories are, yet they have stuck firmly in our minds for the past 30 years and seem just as magical now as they were when we were four. It is these distinct recollections that we've tried to replicate in this book, to provide fantastic themed parties for any budget and help create charming memories for future generations.

Today, one assumes that breaking the bank for every party is the only way to keep children happy, but we

know from experience that this is certainly not true. Going back to the basics is sometimes the best option and all that is needed on your part, is a little imagination and a bit of time spent recollecting your own party memories. Chances are, what worked for you will undoubtedly be a success with your brood too.

After six years on the children's party circuit, organising events for a wealth of clients both at home and abroad, we really know what works. Our Hats & Bells team continue to wow London and the Home Counties families with imaginative and original food. From traditional country kitchens to contemporary town house sitting rooms, every week we witness the children's party scene first hand and try to tackle every event with a sense of humour and total calm.

In this book, we share all our party gems, from those all-important birthday cake recipes, to the simplest table decoration tips. We have focused on consistently popular themes for boys and girls and provided a range of recipes and party games, all of which are destined to impress your guests and herald you as a domestic party queen! We focus on an array of themes (there's ten in all) ranging from Circus, Circus and Wizards and Fairies to that all-important Last-Minute Panic Party. This will enable you to cook and create delicious food for your child's celebration, without breaking the bank or

missing out on all the fun yourself.

When we launched Hats & Bells back in 2007, having noticed a real gap in the market for children's party food, we had no financial backing and no guarantee that our catering venture would actually work. However, we strongly believe that our 'make food fun' philosophy has been the route of our success, combined with addressing the fact that children's food does not have to be bland and boring to be a hit. Taste is, after all, one way in which children experience the world, so what better time to introduce your little guests to the occasional surprise ingredient, than at a party? Don't be scared to add some 'Parmesan snow' to lift your familiar popcorn bags or edible lavender to enliven your homemade shortbread. Even if there are dietary restrictions to take into consideration (something we are very aware of in this modern world of additives and allergies), the key is always to present food in an imaginative and spellbinding way, using the freshest and highest quality ingredients available to you. With today's busy lives and hectic schedules, conjuring up original, stunning and delicious party food cannot always be top of every parent's list but we hope our book will help you make party food easy, stylish and most importantly, fun.

LET'S THROW A PARTY!

We all know that children's parties are big business and have been for some years now. As a parent, the party market can seem overwhelming. It is flooded with hundreds of different options for every single possible category, from entertainers and face-painters to table decorations and personalised cakes. Where, oh where do you start? Today, expectations really do run wild and there is huge pressure to throw the crème de la crème of all parties in order to 'keep up with the Joneses' and to satisfy the birthday boy or girl. Whatever the budget and whatever the vision, a child's party does not and should not be a daunting prospect or a financial struggle for any parent. The key is to do a little forward planning, taking into consideration the following pointers: the time of year you are planning the party; the number of guests you intend on inviting; the budget; the theme; and whether you are expecting a gathering of parents or just children. A little thought before B-Day, will ensure a smooth result, so do spend a few hours chatting through options with another family member, or a friend who has some experience in organising a children's party.

A word of warning about parties. As with any important celebration, it's all too easy to get carried away and before you know it, you've vastly overspent or have run out of time to make everything you wanted before the big day. All this creates stress and stress is not what you need for a good party. Remember, your child will not care about certain things and it's important to rein in any ideas about impressing others; the party is about celebrating your child's birthday and giving him or her a memorable day.

THE THEME

An easy way in to planning a party, is to think about a theme. Most children will have a strong idea about what they would like. Be warned, this choice will probably change four or five times in the run up to the big day, so give your child a cut-off date to finalise their decision! Do not panic if they choose a cartoon character that you are not too familiar with, or if they go down the more commercial route (say, a Disney character), as you can easily adapt it. For example, if he or she asks for Ariel from *The Little Mermaid* you can have a Pirates and Mermaids party, which not only makes it more accessible for you but makes it unisex, keeping everyone happy. In each chapter, we have chosen themes that will work for both girls and boys and a large majority of the recipes are interchangeable with other themes, so do look at different chapters for further inspiration. We have presented the chapters in a loose, chronological order of children's ages, from Teddy Bears' Picnic, which is perfect for toddlers, to Wild, Wild West, which is ideal for 6–12 year-olds.

THE PARTY VENUE

If you don't fancy your home becoming a stomping ground for muddy feet and sticky fingers, or you are worried that you do not have enough space, then there are always venues available to hire. Church or town halls are great alternatives but be sure to make a checklist of what you need from a venue. For example, can the room or hall accommodate all of

your guests? Are the tables and chairs suitable for both children and adults? Can you use the kitchen and is there an oven? Is there parking? Is it possible to decorate the room and play music? Are you allowed to move the furniture around? Lastly, but most importantly, how long is the venue available for and does it match your budget? Do remember that you will need to access the room a good hour before the start of the party, in order to set up decorations, lay tables and begin prepping any food. If you have hired a face-painter or entertainer, they too will need early access, so they can get themselves organised and ready for action. Time-keeping is essential in ensuring a smoothly executed party, so do go through this carefully, allowing enough time for each element.

THE PARTY INVITATIONS

There are so many options for invitations nowadays and it is best to try and send them at least three weeks before your party date. For a simple and quick idea, simply go online. Here you can find hundreds of designs to suit all themes and there are even companies that do free downloads, which you can personalise and print out yourself (see Directory on page 204). At the other end of the spectrum, there are many companies that will design and print elaborate invitations on beautiful paper or card (you can choose the thickness and colour). However, it is a good idea to have a design in mind, as the options can be overwhelming and before you know it, you will leave the meeting even more confused than when you arrived! Finally, you can never go wrong with a homemade invitation and this is a great way of involving the birthday boy or girl and their siblings. It does not matter if each invitation is different but it is probably a good idea for you or another adult to write the essential party details onto each invite to avoid any confusion! When visiting your craft or stationery shop for supplies, think: card, glitter, feathers, sequins, stickers, glue and crayons or felt-tip pens. Add good sized envelopes to this list too; it is important to put these invitations into envelopes, to save book bags from a dusting of glitter!

While every generation seems to be sending or receiving invitations over the internet these days, at Hats & Bells, we are slightly more old-fashioned. While an email is quick and convenient for you, it does seem rather impersonal and there is always a danger that it could end up in a recipient's 'junk' box. If you go down

the traditional route, you can ensure that each invite will reach its rightful owner by handing them out at school or asking the children's teacher to do this for you at the end of the day. Paperless post certainly comes in handy when it comes to chasing replies or sending reminders.

MENU CHOICES

We have given roughly eight recipe ideas for each chapter but when we are advising clients, we normally suggest their choice consists of two mains, two 'bits and bobs' and three sweet choices. (Bits and bobs are smaller savoury items, for example cheesy biscuits or potato skins.) So, with this in mind, feel free to lose a few options but ensure that you make extra of your chosen items. One big tip from us – never go for 'half and half'. For example, if you have 20 guests, do not be tempted to cook just 10 portions of fish goujons and then 10 burgers, as you will find yourself in serious trouble! We have seen clients try this in the past and it never works. Children are led by each other, so if one reaches for the fish, they'll all want fish, leaving you short of one choice but inundated with the other. Make sure you make enough of each item to feed each

ALLERGIES AND INTOLERANCES

If a child has a severe allergy, their parents will usually provide appropriate food for them. If, in very rare cases, they don't offer to do this, do not fret. All large supermarkets now offer a great range of pre-packaged, specialist foods, which are 'free from' most of the common allergens: egg, gluten and dairy. Whenever we are catering for a child with an allergy, we try our best to make their food look as similar as possible to the other food on offer, so they don't feel any different from the other children. If pizza is on the menu, for example, then simply buy a gluten-free base, pile high with your chosen toppings and cut it into the same shape as all the other pizzas. No one will know the difference!

Do be wary when it comes to nut allergies, as they are acutely dangerous and, at times, life-threatening. Do not cater for any nut allergies unless you have full support from the parent of the child or you yourself are fully familiar with this problem. Everyday products, such as flour and sugar usually have 'traces of nut' written on their packaging, so do be very careful. There are a few companies (see Directory on page 204) specialising in nut-free products, which stock appropriate products for kids' parties, so do look into this option if you are given the green light.

child (plus extras). Any leftovers will no doubt be nabbed by a hungry adult, or can be reheated for your supper later.

Another thing to consider, is whether you want to serve all the food together, mixing sweet and savoury, or separately. As the parent and party giver, this is most definitely your prerogative. If you are of the 'it's a party, let them eat cake' group, then go for it and mound the table high with both options. However, if you are keen for a bit of healthy before a bit of naughty, then definitely stagger the food in two stages. This might seem like the boring option but it might please the other parents and it will reduce the likelihood of any serious sugar highs!

BIRTHDAY CAKES

All the cakes we have included here are definitely doable by an amateur baker but if making the birthday cake is one step too far for you, then look no further than your local supermarket or high-street bakery. The range of birthday cakes on offer today is quite astounding and the chances are, you'll be able to find something on the cake aisle to fit your theme and keep your little one happy. Alternatively, if baking the cake is something that you are keen to undertake (but are worried about running out of time), then look into buying a shaped cake tin or mould. Your local party store should stock these in abundance, or look online for inspiration. Number cake tins are a great cheat too; before you have even decorated them they resemble what they should resemble, so there is little room for error! We use just two tried-and-tested sponge recipes for birthday cakes – one white chocolate vanilla and one chocolate. They are easy to put together and anyone can bake them – and their taste cannot be rivalled by packet mixes or similar.

FOOD PRESENTATION

When we started Hats & Bells in 2007, we were both in agreement that food presentation was going to be a major key to our success. Soggy sandwiches and anaemic cookies bunged onto paper plates were not part of our plan and even though this was what was on offer growing up in the 1980s, we felt it was time for a renaissance! Children need to be stimulated and wowed at parties, just like the children were when they entered Willy Wonka's chocolate factory. So, with this film and mantra in mind, we have, over the past few years, tried and tested many different recipes and presentation ideas, to see whether they were met with children's approval.

Crudités are hardly exciting but thread them onto glittery sticks and place them upright in a flowerpot (that is filled with little seashells) and suddenly you are onto a winner! The more fun and extraordinary your food looks, the more curious children become and the more likely they are to eat it. When it comes to presentation equipment, think mini and large flowerpots, buckets, Kilner jars, milk bottles and fun-shaped plates, slates and wooden boards. Add ribbons or raffia around the necks of jars and attach luggage labels, complete with messages or names, scrolled onto them. It is also important to serve little people, little portions, so when it comes to cutting tray cakes, think miniature. Bite-sized cubes of deliciousness, piled high onto plates or in jam jars look fabulous, especially if you scatter them with berries or smashed toffee and finish off with a dusting of icing sugar.

One thing we have noticed at parties, is how excited children get when they are given their 'own' food. Rather than making one large chocolate mousse or lasagne and then simply dolling it out, why not make individual portions in separate ramekins or jars, one for each child? If you are planning on serving just cold food, find some mini boxes that fit your theme and fill each one with the food you have prepared. If you have time, wrap each item in candy striped bags and write each guest's name on a box. Hide these away somewhere cool until needed. The children will love them and they can be packed up a good few hours before the party starts.

FANCY DRESS

Dressing up is an easy way of incorporating your theme into the party but make sure it is clearly signposted on the invitations, so as to avoid any embarrassment. If you can face it, get involved too, even if it is just wearing a cowboy hat or some Dracula teeth. Something token always amuses the children on arrival and you'll be known as a 'super cool' parent for some time. Your child's costume does not need to break the bank and it is

amazing what you can find lying around your house. A man's tie can become a pirate bandana and a floaty scarf can transform a cone of card into a princess hat. A little imagination is all that is needed. Joke and toy shops sell everything from pirate patches and stuffed parrots, to plastic crowns and wands, so do make time for a visit there. Most households have a dressing-up box, so be sure to raid this or at least have it at the ready, in case a guest arrives unprepared.

GAMES AND PRIZES

We have suggested some new and old games in each chapter and it is a good idea to have some prizes at the ready for the winners. Times have certainly changed since we were small and these days, parents offer prizes all through parties and everyone gets them, not just a solitary winner. Some see this as generosity, while others think it over the top! Wherever you stand, kids these days expect sweets in the layers of pass the parcel or as a consolation prize in other games. Whether it is just a tube of toffees or mini loot bags filled with cheap 'cracker' presents (which you can put

together beforehand), make sure you have this area covered. Nobody wants an upset or disappointed child at their party. Popular prizes to consider are: lollipops, mini chocolate bars, small stuffed toys, friendship bracelets, stickers, bouncy balls, bags of marbles and mini packs of cards. Just remember, these presents do not need to be extravagant and should be handed out liberally. Do not feel any pressure to visit Harrods and buy up the entire Play Station or Barbie section! Just because 'Ella's mother did it', does not mean you need to follow suit. Set a budget for this area and stick to it.

PARTY ENTERTAINERS

We have had a great insight into the children's entertainer market since 2007. As we are watching from a completely objective viewpoint, we find it fascinating to see how each company or individual handle different situations and the audience's reaction to them. There is nothing worse than witnessing an entertainer 'lose control' of his/her guests, as he/she then panics, the parent becomes anxious and before you know it, the party snowballs. It is therefore

essential to ask friends or family for recommendations or check children's magazines for positive write-ups. Experience is pivotal in the party world, so if you are unsure of a company's history, do ask the manager basic questions, for your piece of mind. How long have you been established? How many employees do you have and what is the average age of each entertainer? It is a good idea to make a list of what you want from your chosen entertainer. For example, do you want a storyteller or a clown? Do you want them to play games, perform magic or both? Do you want them to help you serve the food at teatime? Be very clear on what you expect from them and make sure you agree a set price before the party. Being hit with a bill for hidden extras at a later date is the last thing you want. The best entertainers can get booked up months in advance, so if you see one you like at another party, book them on the spot to avoid disappointment or send them an email that evening.

THANK YOU NOTES

It's a good idea, if the birthday boy or girl can bear it, to save the present opening until all your guests have left. Then you can sit there, with paper and pen in hand, making a note of who gave your child what. As a parent, you may already be familiar with the painful letter writing process! No child (or grown up) finds it fun but it is worth it in the long run. There is no need to write an essay, just a couple of lines on either a hand-decorated or shop-bought card is all that is needed. If your child is too young to write, you can do it for them and let them doodle their name inside or scribble a picture on the front. For a really thoughtful thank you note (which needs a little bit of forward planning), take a photo of each child at the party, print it out and send it as a postcard to each guest.

our Two Basic sponge Recipes

Hatty's aunt – Diana Tosswill – used to make cakes for children throughout London and to have one of her creations was a real treat. When we started Hats & Bells, she very generously handed over her handwritten notes and delicious sponge cake recipes, which never fail to impress and are 100 per cent foolproof!

WHITE CHOCOLATE VANILLA SPONGE

Something a little different from your average sponge cake. The white chocolate is very subtle, not too sweet and is delicious combined with the vanilla.

Makes 1 x 20cm x 9cm round cake or 2 x 25 x 34cm rectangular cakes or 42 cupcakes

100g white chocolate

225g self-raising flour

225g caster sugar

3 heaped teaspoons baking powder

5 tablespoons water

6 tablespoons sunflower oil

1 tablespoon vanilla extract

6 eggs, separated

Grease and line your chosen tin(s) with baking parchment or place 42 paper cupcake cases on four baking trays. Preheat the oven to 180°C/gas mark 4.

Melt the chocolate in a heatproof bowl over a pan of barely simmering water, making sure the bowl doesn't touch the water. Put all the dry ingredients in a mixing bowl. Add the water, oil and vanilla extract and add the egg yolks. Beat well until all the dry ingredients become incorporated. Add the melted chocolate to the mixture and beat again.

In a separate bowl beat the egg whites until stiff but not dry. Add the egg whites to the mixture and mix carefully until well combined. Pour the mixture into the cake tins (or cupcake cases) and bake for 25–30 minutes (15 minutes for the cupcakes) or until springy to the touch and shrinking away from the edges of the tin.

Leave in the tins for 5–10 minutes and then turn out onto wire racks, carefully peeling off the baking parchment off the cakes.

CHOCOLATE SPONGE

Everyone should have an easy chocolate sponge recipe 'up their sleeve' and this is ours at Hats & Bells. Rich, divine and simply perfect for that special celebration cake.

Makes 1 x 20cm x 9cm round cake or 2 x 25 x 34cm rectangular cakes or 42 cupcakes

100g dark chocolate (minimum 60 per cent cocoa solids)

225g self-raising flour

225g caster sugar

3 heaped teaspoons baking powder

3 heaped tablespoons cocoa powder, sifted

6 tablespoons water

6 tablespoons sunflower oil

6 eggs, separated

Grease and line your chosen tin(s) with baking parchment or place 42 paper cupcake cases on four baking trays. Preheat the oven to 180°C/gas mark 4.

Melt the chocolate in a heatproof bowl over a pan of barely simmering water, making sure the bowl doesn't touch the water. Put all the dry ingredients into a large mixing bowl. Add the water, oil and egg yolks and beat until well combined. Add the melted chocolate to the mixture and beat again.

In a separate bowl, beat the egg whites until stiff but not dry. Add the egg whites to the mixture and mix gently until well combined. Pour the mixture into the cake tins (or cupcake cases) and bake for 25–30 minutes (15 minutes for the cupcakes) or until springy to the touch and shrinking away from the edges of the tin.

Leave in the tins for 5–10 minutes and then turn out onto wire racks, carefully peeling off the baking parchment off the cakes.

our Basic Icings

Initially, we both found the idea of icing a birthday cake pretty intimidating. However, with a bit a practice and realising that mistakes can easily be 'patched up', the task is now less daunting and rather more enjoyable. Before you start, it is a good idea to map out your design on a piece of paper first.

WHITE BUTTER ICING

Butter icing is simple to make, easy to spread and forms a great base for sticking on extra decorations and covering up a slightly less than perfect cake.

Makes 500g
225g unsalted butter, softened
325g icing sugar, sifted

Put the butter and icing sugar in a bowl and beat hard until the mixture becomes white.
  You can add one teaspoon of any of the following: vanilla extract, lemon juice or orange juice for flavouring if you like.

CHOCOLATE BUTTER ICING

A chocolate version of the vanilla butter icing. Perfect for any serious chocoholics who want to indulge in a double chocolate overload! Delicious with vanilla cakes too.

Makes 500g
225g unsalted butter, softened
325g icing sugar, sifted
55g cocoa powder, sifted
1–2 tablespoons semi-skimmed milk

Put the butter, icing sugar and cocoa and 1 tablespoon of milk in a bowl and beat hard until the mixture is smooth and creamy. Beat in another tablespoon of milk if necessary.

CHOCOLATE FUDGE ICING

This fudge icing is hard to beat when it comes to taste. Rich and velvety smooth, it is our number one bestseller and is perfect for holding cakes together (or what we call, 'containing the crumb').

Makes 800g
200ml semi-skimmed milk
225g unsalted butter
900g icing sugar, sifted
110g cocoa powder, sifted

Heat the milk and butter in a saucepan over a low heat until the butter has melted.
  Put the icing sugar and cocoa into a large mixing bowl and beat in the milk and butter mixture. Beat hard until perfectly smooth. Leave to cool. As it cools it will become stiffer and easy to spread.

APRICOT GLAZE

This is mostly used as a 'glue' for sticking fondant icing onto birthday cakes or biscuits. Takes just seconds to make up.

Makes 100ml
125g apricot jam
1 tablespoon water

Heat the jam and water gently in a small non-stick saucepan, stirring occasionally until the jam has melted.
  Remove from the heat and strain the jam mixture through a sieve into a clean bowl.

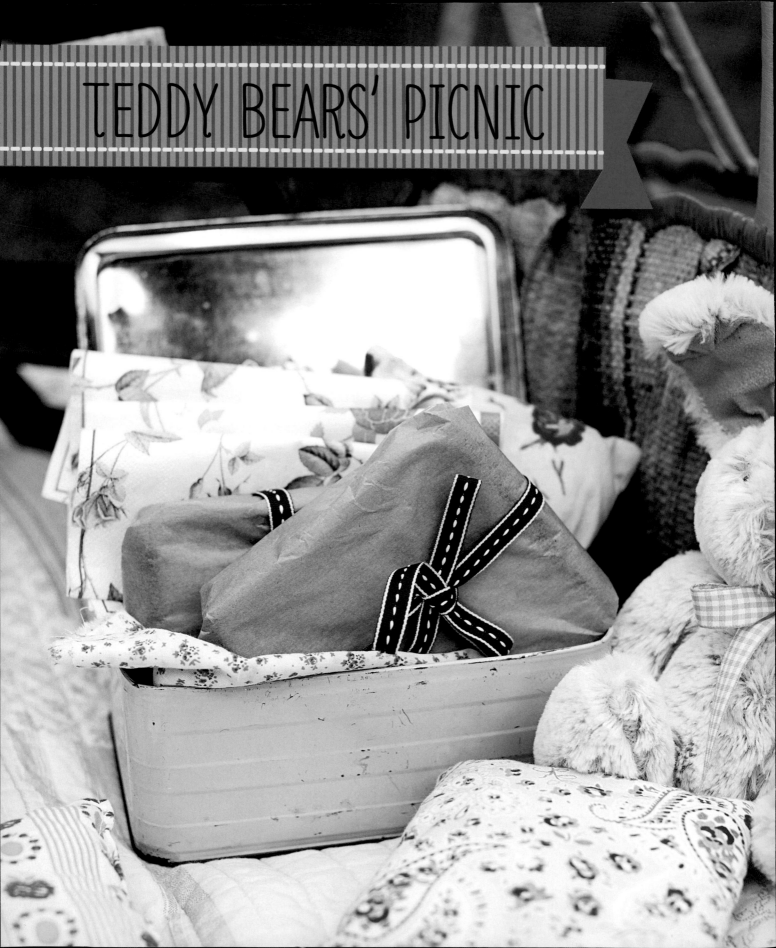

TEDDY BEARS' PICNIC

TEDDY BEARS' PICNIC

If you go down to the woods today, you're sure of a big surprise! This theme is especially popular with toddlers and those children who have birthdays in late spring and summer. As the weather can be unpredictable, just be prepared to transfer your outdoor party indoors. Everyone loves a picnic and whether it's inside or outside doesn't matter a jot. Lay all your rugs, cushions and hampers on the floor and snuggle down together.

Ask your guests to each bring along their favourite teddy bear and make name tags out of luggage labels for their furry friends. Choose a sheltered spot in your garden, local park or woods, ideally one that is naturally contained by hedges or trees. Hang pretty bunting and dot paper windmills and lanterns around the picnic area. If you're really going to town, then why not make little posies of wild flowers and stick them in old honey pots for a pretty and easy table decoration or scatter lavender sprigs all around the picnic area, for a wonderful, magical smell. (You can buy dried lavender online, all year round.) Think wicker baskets, checked tablecloths or rugs, party hats and perhaps a balloon to tie to each bear's paw. Why not leave a couple of adults in charge of setting up the picnic, while you meet and greet your guests? Then embark on a treasure hunt with the other parents and children, ending up at the already prepared picnic spot.

Toddlers do not need as much entertaining as older children, so just have a few traditional games at the ready. For instance, pass the parcel, musical bumps and hide and seek are all easy games for this age group to participate in but do remember to pack some music that will play en plein air! You might find that not all the children want to participate in the games – do not worry! Most parents for this age group will stay for the duration of the party, so there will always be someone to help look after any stragglers!

When it comes to the food, the mantra for this theme is... preparation, preparation, preparation. In this chapter, you'll find our simple yet original picnic ideas that can all be made and packed well ahead of time, making your life on the day so much easier. For the ultimate Teddy Bears' Picnic, wrap food in spotty handkerchiefs tied with ribbon and give your guests mini baskets instead of paper plates.

Recently we hid mini-jars of honey around the garden and before the children left they and their bears had to go and find their own pot. This was the perfect 'going home' present for all the teddies! For the children, fill little gift boxes or colourful bags with gummy bears (which can be bought online for a reasonable price) and tie them with paw-print ribbon. One thing is for sure, by the time six o'clock comes you'll have some very tired (but very happy) little teddy bears...

ted's pea pots

MAKES 8 ⭐

These little pots are deliciously fresh and easily transportable. We have used cream cheese to ensure a stiffer dip for the crudités to stand up in but you could use crème fraîche or natural yogurt, if you prefer. Make these the day before and just leave in the fridge until you're packing up your picnic.

Place the peas in a pan of boiling water and cook on the hob for 8 minutes or until tender. Drain and leave to cool.

Place the peas in a blender, add the mint leaves and pulse until smooth. (If you do not have a blender, gently mash the mixture, using the back of a fork. The result will be more textured but still delicious!)

In a separate bowl loosen the cream cheese slightly using a wooden spoon before adding the lemon juice. Mix together gently.

Tip in the blended peas and stir until well combined.

Divide the dip between eight pots, cover and leave in the fridge until needed. Just before serving, stand the crudités upright in each pot and serve.

you will need

200g frozen peas

4 mint leaves

250g cream cheese

2 tablespoons lemon juice

fresh crudités of your choice, such as carrot batons, sugar snap peas, mini corn and cucumber sticks

monsieur teddy

SERVES 8 ★

Sandwiches are always going to be a hit at a picnic and, it seems that, when you cut them into shapes they disappear very quickly! We have made these Monsieur Teddies with cheese but cream cheese, ham, honey and jam are all crowd pleasers.

Cut the crusts off the white bread and spread them with a thin layer of butter and then a thin layer of pesto. Add a slice of Red Leicester cheese and sandwich together.

Repeat this process with the brown bread and Cheddar cheese.

In the centre of each sandwich round, cut out a teddy shape using a teddy-shaped cookie cutter. Being careful not to break the sandwich push the teddy shape out.

On two large serving plates, alternate white teddies with brown for a pleasing array.

To keep the sandwiches as fresh as possible, wrap them in greaseproof paper and tie with string ready for your picnic.

you will need

16 slices of medium sliced white bread

250g spreadable butter

4 tablespoons pesto

8 slices of Red Leicester

16 slices of medium sliced brown bread

8 slices of Cheddar (either mild or medium)

Ready Teddy Goo Goo

SERVES 16

This was a favourite of both of ours growing up in the 1980s and we make no apology for this amazing concoction of sugary happiness! We have introduced these to a number of our clients, who have begged us for the recipe… so here it is. Be warned, you may want to restrict these to one per child!

Line a 24 x 20cm baking tray with baking parchment.

In a large saucepan, melt the marshmallows, soft toffees and butter together over a low heat. Once melted and smooth, remove from the heat and leave to cool slightly. Add the Rice Krispies and gently stir together. Spoon the Goo Goo mixture into the tin and immediately put the tin in the fridge to set.

Meanwhile, chop the Mars bars into small pieces and put into a non-stick saucepan. Add the milk and melt together over a low heat, stirring occasionally. Once melted and smooth remove from the heat.

Remove the cakes from the fridge and using a teaspoon, casually drizzle the Mars mixture over the Goo Goo cakes. Place back in the fridge for at least an hour before serving cut into squares.

For the goo goo

100g marshmallows
100g soft toffees
150g unsalted butter
200g Rice Krispies

For the topping

3 x 58g Mars bars
2 tablespoons semi-skimmed milk

gingerbread ted

Honest and gorgeously old-fashioned, these heavenly biscuits will be swiped by both adults and children, so make sure there are plenty. Have fun using different cookie cutters to suit any occasion or wrap in little party bags to give as 'going home' party treats.

Preheat the oven to 190°C/gas mark 5. Line a baking tray with baking parchment.

Mix the flour, ginger, cinnamon, cloves and bicarbonate of soda with the butter until the mixture resembles breadcrumbs.

Add the sugar, syrup and egg to the mixture and beat together using a wooden spoon until it comes together in one large ball. Wrap in clingfilm and leave to chill in the fridge for 15 minutes.

Place the dough onto a lightly floured surface and using a rolling pin, roll out until approx. 5mm thick.

Using a bear-shaped cookie cutter (approx. 3.5 x 4cm), stamp out the shapes and place on the lined baking tray.

Bake for 8–12 minutes or until golden in colour.

Remove from the oven and let the biscuits harden for 5 minutes before removing them from the baking tray and carefully transferring them onto a wire rack. Leave to cool for 1 hour.

Dust the work surface with icing sugar and roll out the white fondant icing block to 2mm in thickness.

Take your bear cutter and stamp out an icing teddy. Brush a little water on one side of the biscuit and stick onto a Gingerbread Ted. Repeat for the remaining gingerbread shapes.

Using a tube of writing icing, draw on a smiley face.

Squeeze a small dot of icing onto one side of a Smartie or coloured chocolate and gently place down the centre of the Gingerbread Ted's tummy. We usually allow three chocolates per ted. Repeat this process for all the biscuits and leave to set for an hour before serving.

you will need

250g plain flour, sifted, plus extra for dusting

1 teaspoon ground ginger

1 teaspoon ground cinnamon

1/2 teaspoon ground cloves

1 teaspoon bicarbonate of soda

125g unsalted butter, softened

170g light brown sugar

3 tablespoons golden syrup

1 medium egg

for the decoration

icing sugar, for dusting

500g white ready-made fondant icing

tubes of coloured writing icing

75g Smarties or other small coloured chocolates

Jam Pot Jelly Jars

SERVES 8

It might sound old-fashioned but jelly and custard is still as popular as ever at children's parties. Every now and then we spot the odd parent subtly tucking into this nostalgic treat! Packed with delicious berries, these are simply perfect for any picnic, just remember to pack the spoons!

Make 600ml of lemon jelly according to the packet instructions.

Place a small handful of blueberries in the bottom of the eight jam jars in just a single layer. Pour the lemon jelly over the blueberries so that it comes to a third of the way up the height of the jar. Repeat with the remaining jam jars and put in the fridge to set for 2 hours.

Make 600ml of raspberry jelly according to the packet instructions.

Take the lemon jellies out of the fridge and scatter a handful of raspberries over the set jelly. Pour the raspberry jelly over the raspberries, two-thirds of the way up the height of the jar. Repeat this process for the remaining jam jars and return to the fridge to set for a further 2 hours.

Once the jellies have set, pour the custard up to the bottom of the neck of the jar. Put in the fridge to cool completely before topping with a strawberry slice and placing a jam jar lid on top of each jar.

Remove from the fridge and pack them safely in your picnic basket, with some spoons, ready for the feast.

you will need

135g packet lemon jelly
100g blueberries
135g packet raspberry jelly
100g raspberries
400g ready-made custard
8 strawberry slices, to decorate

turkey in Blankets

We are often asked for new pork-free party food ideas and came up with these, which have been hugely popular. They are a variation of a traditional sausage roll but instead of pork we use turkey mince, jazzed up with some sun-dried tomatoes.

Preheat the oven to 200°C/gas mark 6. Line a baking tray with baking parchment.

Put the turkey mince into a bowl and add the sun-dried tomatoes, fresh basil, dried herbs and season.

Break one of the eggs into the turkey mixture and using a wooden spoon combine the ingredients.

Lay the pastry sheet horizontally onto a lightly floured surface and cut it into three even slices, from top to bottom.

Split the turkey mixture into three and roll each portion into a sausage shape using your hands. Lay one portion of the mixture along the edge of one side of each pastry rectangle.

Beat the remaining egg and, using a pastry brush, brush over each rectangle on the turkey-free side and then lift the pastry over and seal it as carefully as possible.

Using scissorts or a sharp knife, cut each long roll into eight small rolls and place on the baking tray. Brush with the remaining egg and cook for 25–30 minutes or until golden brown and cooked through.

Remove from the oven and transfer to a wire rack to cool. These are best served warm. They can be stored in an airtight container for up to two days and reheated at 200°C/gas mark 6 for 10 minutes before serving.

you will need

450g turkey mince

280g sun-dried tomatoes, chopped

a handful of fresh basil, finely chopped

1 teaspoon dried mixed herbs

salt and freshly ground black pepper

2 medium eggs

flour, for dusting

320g ready-rolled puff pastry sheet

Teddy Bear cake

SERVES 10–12 ⋯⋯⋯⋯⋯⋯⋯⋯⋯⋯⋯⋯⋯⋯⋯⋯⋯★

However nervous you may be about undertaking the birthday cake challenge, this teddy face cake will soon give you confidence. It really is super-easy, takes very little time and will be a hit with all your little guests. Other cakes to consider for this theme include a Teddy Bears' Picnic scene, a picnic hamper or flowers, ladybirds or butterflies.

Carefully centre one sponge on a round 30.5cm cake board. Cover the cake in a thin layer of chocolate fudge icing to contain the crumbs and to act as a glue for the additional cake pieces.

Take the second sponge cake and using pastry cutters stamp out two 7cm circles and one 10cm circle.

Place the large circle (the teddy's nose) 3cm up from the bottom of the sponge on the cake board.

Cut one third off the bottom of the two smaller circles in a slight curve (we use the edges of the pastry cutters) and place them at the top of the cake (these are the teddy's ears). Cover the nose and ears in a layer of chocolate fudge icing and leave to set for 1 hour.

Next, either spread a layer of chocolate butter icing over the entire cake, smoothing over with a wet palette knife or, for a great furry effect, use a grass icing nozzle with an icing bag. Don't be afraid of nozzles and icing bags, they are easy to use.

you will need

2 x 20cm round Chocolate Sponge Cakes (see recipe page 16)

400g Chocolate Fudge Icing (see recipe page 17)

500g Chocolate Butter Icing (see recipe page 17)

100g light brown ready-made fondant icing

icing sugar, for dusting

2 giant white chocolate buttons (approx. 3–4cm)

1 small black icing pen

80g jelly beans (optional)

edible flowers, to decorate (optional)

Lay the light brown fondant icing on a smooth work surface dusted with icing sugar and roll out the icing until it is about 1cm thick.

Using pastry cutlers, as before, stamp out a 10cm disc and one 5cm disc.

Carefully place the large disc on top of the teddy's nose. Cut the smaller disc in half and then trim the bottom of each half so they are slightly curved (see right). Place the half discs into the centre of the teddy's ears, with the curved edge at the join of the ear and the head (see photo on previous page).

Place the two giant white chocolate buttons (the teddy's eyes) above the nose and use the black icing pen to draw two black semicircles on the chocolate buttons.

Then draw a 2.5cm rounded triangle at the top of the nose section. The point of the triangle should be facing down. Ice a straight line down from the point, about 5.5cm in length, ending in a lovely semicircle smile.

To add a bit of colour, you can scatter a couple of handfuls of jelly beans and a few edible flowers (pansies look wonderful) around the cake before serving.

Bears-Love-Honey Shake

SERVES 8

This super-sweet fruity shake can be whipped up several hours ahead of serving and kept covered in a jug in the fridge. If the mixture is a bit too thick for your little ones, just add more milk until the ideal consistency is reached.

Put the bananas, milk and 200g of the crushed honeycomb into a blender and whizz for 30 seconds or until smooth.

Pour into a large jug, cover and chill in the fridge before packing up for your picnic.

When ready, pour the shake into eight small glasses and sprinkle with a little of the reserved honeycomb before serving to your guests.

you will need

3 ripe bananas
1 litre semi-skimmed milk, chilled
250g crushed honeycomb

FARMYARD FUN

FARMYARD FUN

This theme is particularly popular with the younger age groups and is perfect for all animal-loving children. Long wooden benches and tables covered with red gingham tablecloths will set the scene, as will a few mini hay bales, which you can pick up from your local pet shop. Line tables with glass vases (filled with a little water) and a few swimming rubber ducks. You could always add a little blue food colouring to the water to get a real pond effect. These are always a great talking point and make a refreshing change from chocolate or sweet table decorations.

For the rest of the party area, place little baskets of fresh apples on side tables and borrow any appropriate stuffed animals from your offspring and sit them at the party table, as well as grouped in other areas.

If your budget includes helium balloons, then you're spoilt for choice. Think foil animals, cowprint patterns and horse shoes or simply keep to primary colours and draw on your own designs with a permanent pen.

Such a simple theme lends itself to those fabulously old-fashioned games, such as the egg and spoon race, in which participants must balance an egg upon a spoon and race with it to the finishing line, or Stuck in the Mud where one child is the 'tagger' and once a child has been tagged by them they must stand still with their arms and legs outstretched. They can only be freed when another child crawls between their legs without being caught by the 'tagger'. Just make sure you have lots of different coloured ribbons or rosettes to hand out as prizes.

Younger children are blissfully happy entertaining themselves, so why not set up a craft table. Playdough is always popular, as is colouring in printouts of various animal and farmyard scenes.

This country-related theme offers plenty of opportunities for pretty serving ideas. Flowerpots, Kilner jars and little hessian bags, tied with gingham ribbon all make cute alternatives to plates and bowls.

If an outing to the zoo sounds too much like hard work, how about bringing the animals to your home? Swap the traditional party clown for an animal keeper, who will bring along rabbits, hamsters, parrots and many more, to keep your guests amused. Be sure to specify the exact age group with the company, as boxes of snakes and spiders might not go down too well with toddlers, or their parents for that matter!

If you are feeling extravagant, hobby horses make excellent and appropriate 'going home' presents. You can have a big bucket of them by the door ready to hand out at the end of the party. For a cheaper alternative, fill hessian bags with homemade popcorn (see page 135) and stick labels reading 'chicken feed' on the front of each bag. Why not attach a mini chick to the bag for a fun and colourful extra?

chicken porky pies

MAKES 10

Thank goodness for ready-made puff pastry. Forget wasting hours in the kitchen kneading away Mrs Beeton-style! These cute pies will have everyone talking and they can be prepped a day before the party, up until the eggwash stage.

Preheat the oven to 180°C/gas mark 4. Grease ten standard-sized ramekins and set aside. Melt the butter in a saucepan over a low heat. Stir in the flour and mix until combined. Remove the pan from the heat and gradually stir in the milk to create a smooth paste. Return the pan to the heat and using a hand whisk, stir the mixture constantly to prevent any lumps. Once the sauce has thickened (this will take a good 5 minutes) and is smooth and bubbling, remove from the heat.

Add the diced chicken breast, sweetcorn and salt and pepper to the white sauce and mix together.

Unwrap the pastry sheet onto a lightly floured surface. Cut out ten 8cm circles and ten 2.5cm circles using a pastry cutter, followed by 20 triangles with sides of 1.5cm.

Place 2 large heaped tablespoons of the chicken mixture into a ramekin and top with the large pastry circle. Brush the pastry with the beaten egg and place the small circle onto the centre of the large circle and two triangles per ramekin for the pig's ears. Re-brush the top of the pie with the beaten egg.

Make two holes through the small circle, which will let the steam leave the pie and also create the pig's nostrils.

Place the ramekins on a large baking tray and bake for 20 minutes or until the pastry is golden brown and risen.

Just before serving, halve the olives and place two halves on the pig's face to make eyes. Place each ramekin on a plate and surround with garden peas or Little Gem lettuce and serve hot.

you will need

25g salted butter, plus extra for greasing

25g plain flour, plus extra for dusting

600ml semi-skimmed milk

3 cooked chicken breasts, diced

198g can sweetcorn, drained

salt and freshly ground black pepper

320g ready-rolled puff pastry sheet

1 medium egg, beaten

10 black olives

peas or Little Gem lettuce, to serve

Rooster's Roulade

SERVES 8

A very different take on a baguette, this can be made hours before the party and left in the fridge to set – the longer the better. Make sure you use a sharp knife to cut the roulade to ensure a smooth finish. Dipping your knife in a little hot water will help with this. The filling is totally versatile, so feel free to add anything to your cream cheese mixture.

Slice off both ends of the baguette. Using a long thin knife and working from both ends, hollow out the baguette, leaving about a 1.5cm thick crust all around.

With a spatula, beat the cream cheese until smooth and then add the rest of the ingredients. Mix together until combined.

Working from both ends, fill the baguette with the cream cheese mixture, packing the filling in tightly. Be sure to roll your sleeves up for this bit, as it can get a little messy! If you prefer, you could always fill a piping bag with the mixture and pipe it into the baguette. Just make sure the hole in the bag is big enough for all the little bits to get through.

Wrap the baguette up tightly with clingfilm, twisting at both ends and place in the fridge for at least 3 hours or for up to two days.

When you are ready to serve, take the roulade out of the fridge, unwrap the clingfilm and using a sharp knife, slice the baguette into 1.5cm thick slices and pile high on a chopping board.

Top with edible pansies or a basil sprig for a pretty finish.

you will need

- 30cm white or brown baguette
- 250g cream cheese
- 10 slices of honey-roasted ham, finely chopped
- 80g cherry tomatoes, diced
- 1 Little Gem lettuce, finely chopped
- 80g cucumber, deseeded and diced
- salt and freshly ground black pepper
- edible pansies or basil sprig, to garnish

cheesy Farmyard Friends

★

These delicious melt-in-the-mouth morsels are irresistible and look fabulous cut into different animal shapes. You can find just about any shaped cutter online or in good cake and sugar craft shops so start building your collection today. For this recipe your animal cutters need to be about 5–6cm across. These cheesy biscuits are completely versatile and you can add different herbs, spices and hard cheeses, depending on how extravagant your child's taste buds are. This is our favourite combination and a good place to start.

Preheat the oven to 180°C/gas mark 4. Line two baking trays with baking parchment.

Combine the dry ingredients with the butter in a bowl. You can use a wooden spoon but the best technique is rubbing everything together using your fingers. It will feel like the ingredients won't come together, but keep going and it will all form a dough ball eventually. If you prefer, you can use a food processor.

Roll the dough onto a lightly floured surface until it is about 5mm thick.

Cut out the farm animal shapes with the animal cutters and lay them on the lined baking trays.

Bake for 10–15 minutes or until they are golden brown.

Remove from the oven and leave to cool on a wire rack before serving in little jam jars or baskets.

you will need

100g Cheddar, grated
25g Parmesan, grated
75g self-raising flour, plus extra for dusting
50g salted butter, softened

farmers' muffins

MAKES 24

Delicious and nutritious and a brilliant way of getting in your child's five-a-day. These moreish muffins are best served warm but can be reheated in a moderate oven for 10–15 minutes to revive them.

Preheat the oven to 200°C/gas mark 6. Grease two 12-hole mini muffin trays.

Fry the pancetta for 6–8 minutes or until golden and crispy. Remove from the pan with a slotted spoon and set aside on kitchen paper.

Combine the flour, baking powder, bicarbonate of soda, salt and two-thirds of the cheese in a large bowl.

In a separate bowl, mix the beaten eggs, melted butter and buttermilk. Pour the egg mixture over the dry ingredients and stir until just combined.

Gently fold in the cooked pancetta along with the grated courgette. Be careful not to overmix, as this will result in tough muffins.

Spoon the batter equally between the muffin holes, filling generously to just below the rim. Scatter over the remaining cheese and bake for 15–20 minutes or until golden and risen.

Remove from the oven and leave to stand in the tins for 5 minutes before removing the muffins.

Put the mini muffins into little hessian bags and place on the table. These will not only keep them warm but will have the kids guessing about the secret contents.

you will need

200g pancetta, cubed
250g plain flour
2 teaspoons baking powder
½ teaspoon bicarbonate of soda
pinch of salt
200g medium Cheddar, grated
2 medium eggs, beaten
50g unsalted butter, melted
250ml buttermilk
1 small courgette, peeled and grated

chocolate birds' nests

MAKES 12

These sticky, chocolate cornflake clusters are one of our first party food memories. Enclosed in a flowery paper muffin case, finished with some crunchy silver balls… what's not to like? Here we have used cornflakes and mini chocolate eggs but jelly beans also make very convincing birds' eggs. Even though they're easy and quick to make, they're nevertheless impressive and loved by everyone.

Line a 12-hole muffin tray with muffin cases and set aside.

Place the butter, chocolate and golden syrup in a large non-stick pan and slowly melt over a low heat, stirring occasionally. Be sure not to let the chocolate burn.

Once melted and smooth, take off the heat and add the cornflakes. Combine until all the flakes are covered in chocolate before dividing between the 12 cases.

Top with the mini chocolate eggs or jelly beans and a sprinkling of edible glitter and put in the fridge to set for an hour.

A great way to serve these is to rest them on little hay nests. Take a small handful of hay and shape into a bird's nest, making a small dent in the middle. Rest the cakes onto the nests (about three to each nest) and dot down the table. Feel free to add some little fluffy chicks for extra wow.

you will need

50g unsalted butter

110g dark chocolate (minimum 50 per cent cocoa solids), broken into small pieces

4 tablespoons golden syrup

90g cornflakes

jelly beans or mini chocolate eggs and edible glitter, to decorate

marshmallow sheep Biscuits

A delicious traditional shortbread base, smothered with melted chocolate and squidgy marshmallows. These biscuits are a real showstopper and look divine dotted down a green tablecloth, grazing!

Preheat oven to 180°C/gas mark 4. Line two baking trays with baking parchment.

Cream together the butter, sugar and vanilla extract and add the egg. Beat until light and fluffy.

Sift together the cocoa, flour and baking powder and stir into the creamed mixture thoroughly.

Using your hands, form the mixture into a ball and place on a lightly floured surface. Take a rolling pin and roll the dough onto a lightly floured work surface until it is approx. 5mm thick.

Using a sheep cookie cutter (ours was approx. 6cm across), cut out the sheep and place on the baking trays. Bake for 10–12 minutes or until the surface appears dry.

Remove from the oven and let the biscuits harden for 5 minutes before carefully transferring them to a wire rack. Leave to cool for 1 hour.

Cut the mini marshmallows in half and set aside.

Melt the chocolate in a heatproof bowl over a pan of barely simmering water, making sure the bowl doesn't touch the water.

Using a palette knife spread a thin layer of chocolate over the top of the biscuits. Stick the marshmallow bits onto the melted chocolate (cut-side down), leaving only the head uncovered.

Leave the chocolate and marshmallows to set for about 1 hour before serving.

you will need

150g salted butter, softened
200g golden caster sugar
1 teaspoon vanilla extract
1 large egg
80g cocoa powder
220g plain flour, plus extra for dusting
1 teaspoon baking powder

To decorate

240g white mini marshmallows
200g milk or dark chocolate

Farmyard Cake

This farmyard cake is the perfect opportunity to practise your icing modelling skills. The mud puddle adds a bit of humour and you can include as many animals as you wish. If you don't want to make the fondant animals yourself, you can buy them from cake supply shops (see Directory on page 204) or use toys (just remember to remove these before cutting the cake!). Alternatively you could just focus on your child's favourite animal in 2D or 3D form, or go for a classic tractor cake.

Using a ruler, measure an equal height halfway up the cake and insert at least four toothpicks horizontally and evenly spaced just below the measured spot. Cut the cake with a serrated knife just above the toothpicks.

Carefully lift the top half off the cake and place the bottom half of the sponge centrally on a round 30.5cm cake board, securing in place with a dab of chocolate fudge icing.

Take three heaped tablespoons of chocolate fudge icing and spread it evenly over the sponge cake on the board, before carefully replacing the top half of the cake.

Cover the whole cake in a thin layer of chocolate fudge icing to contain the crumbs and create a smooth base for the fondant icing. Leave to set for an hour at room temperature.

Dust the work surface with icing sugar and gently roll out the green fondant icing, until it is approx. 1cm thick and large enough to cover the top and sides of the cake.

Place the icing across the top of the cake and with lightly sugared hands, gently smooth the icing down the sides. Carefully trim any excess icing with a sharp knife.

Next, roll out the brown fondant icing on a work surface dusted with icing sugar until 1cm thick. Then cut out nine 7 x 1.5cm rectangles.

you will need

1 x 20cm round Chocolate Sponge Cake (see recipe page 16)

800g Chocolate Fudge Icing (see recipe page 17)

icing sugar, for dusting

500g green ready-made fondant icing

150g brown ready-made fondant icing

100ml Apricot Glaze (see recipe page 17)

50g pink ready-made fondant icing

1 strawberry bootlace (optional)

1 small black icing pen

Brush one side of each of the rectangles with apricot glaze and place them vertically around the sides of the cake, with a 4.5cm gap between each one.

Re-roll the leftover brown fondant icing, again to a 1cm thickness but this time, cut out 20 rectangles (4.5 x 0.5cm).

As before, brush one side of the rectangle with apricot glaze and place two horizontally between each vertical rectangle and one 0.5cm from the top and the other 0.5cm from the bottom, creating a fence effect. There will be one gap between the vertical rectangles, which will be approx. 13.5cm. Leave this empty to represent the gate into the field.

Re-roll out the last bit of brown fondant icing and cut out a puddle shape.

Brush one side of the mud puddle with apricot glaze and place it on the top of the cake. If you would prefer, you can make a mud puddle by simply using the Chocolate Fudge Icing.

The top of the cake can be as animal-tastic as you like but we definitely find that pigs are the easiest to make, so perhaps start with those. Dust your hands with icing sugar and roll a small bit of the pink fondant icing into a round ball (about 2cm) with no cracks or lines in the surface – this will be the pig's face. To make the pig's body, roll out an oblong approx. 3.5cm long in your hands.

Dip a small paintbrush in a little water and stick the face to the body. Next, make the snout by making a tiny ball of icing and flattening it between your fingers and attaching it to the face with a dab of water. The nostrils can be made by pricking the snout with a toothpick. The ears are little triangles of icing and the tail can be made out of more pink fondant icing or strawberry bootlaces. Next, make four legs with little 0.5cm cubes of the pink icing and attach to the body with some water. We'd suggest using a black icing pen to dot on the eyes.

Once you have made your desired amount of pigs, brush the bottoms of the pig's hooves with apricot glaze and have them slap bang in the muddy puddle! (If you have used the chocolate fudge icing instead of the fondant you do not need any apricot glaze.) Cut one pig in half and then stick it bottom up in the puddle (and perhaps one head up). Watch and enjoy the giggles as the party guests spot the pig enjoying a muddy bath just a bit too much!

Fizzy orchard squash

SERVES 8

Bubbly and refreshing, this will tickle your guests' taste buds and leave them wanting more. Serve with plenty of crushed ice and top with a few fresh blackberries.

Pour the apple juice, sparkling water and lemon juice into a large jug and gently stir with a spoon.

Divide the squash between the glasses or bottles and top with a few blackberries.

you will need

900ml cloudy apple juice, chilled

300ml sparkling water, chilled

1 tablespoon lemon juice

100g fresh blackberries

Wizards and Fairies

Wizards and Fairies

agic knows no bounds – just look at the success of Harry Potter! This is a popular theme for both boys and girls and one which will work indoors and out, so take your pick. Purple and silver seem to be the go to colours for these parties and anything that glitters and shines is an absolute must, as are strings of fairy lights. Online party shops stock a great variety of metallic decorations and iridescent shooting stars look fabulous hanging from ceilings or trees, depending on your ambience. Mix and match paper ball lanterns (we love the 50cm size) for a colourful display running up a garden path or dotted around the room and make sure you have endless mini bottles of fairy dust and confetti to sprinkle over surfaces.

If you're able to make the party room dark, glow sticks and wands never cease to amaze little ones, so make sure you have a large cauldron of these for your guests to pick up and play with. (Why not add some plastic lizards and bugs to the cauldron too, for a surprise?)

Every wizard or fairy needs a hat – as always these can be bought fairly cheaply online but you can make them easily enough too; in fact, you can prepare the bases and get your guests to decorate their own at the start of the party while everyone's arriving. Create a cone-shaped hat from sheets of multicoloured card and roll each piece into a cone. Decorations to have at hand are obviously glitter glue pens, glitter, feathers and perhaps themed or glow-in-the-dark stickers. For any fairies that might be lurking, a pair of fairy wings is an absolute must, so make sure you have a couple of spares for anyone who might arrive without their wings!

Decorate the table with little bottles of Pixie's Potion (see page 65) and flower petals or pot pourri. Old-fashioned, flowery teacups, (which can be picked up cheaply from charity shops), make a pretty addition and are great for serving popping candy. For place settings, why not print off magic spells and fairy poems in a tiny font size on brown paper then scatter a few magnifying glasses down the table, so that the guests can read the messages or spells. Another idea that works well is to give mini decks of playing cards or oversized gold coins to each of the guests, so that they can practise their sleight of hand tricks on their friends and family.

For an extra-special treat, some of our clients hire chocolate fountains but these are kept locked away in a secret place until the party tea has finished! If you want to follow their lead, then fill different-sized jars and vases with marshmallows, pretzels, fresh berries and mini flapjacks, for the ultimate chocolate extravaganza and at its unveiling, why not light some giant sparklers for a bit of extra razzamatazz.

A magician is a great addition to a wizards and fairies party but be sure to book well ahead and check that they can entertain your age group and fit within your budget. It is always a good idea to meet or at least have a detailed telephone conversation with any party entertainer if you can, unless of course you have seen their work at other parties or they come highly recommended from a friend. Face-painters are another popular addition, so again, ask friends for recommendations or failing that, visit online parent chat rooms or flick through local magazines or newspapers for ideas and inspiration.

Games to consider are 'Sugar Plum Says', which is basically Simon Says where one player takes the role of 'Simon' and issues instructions, usually physical such as 'hop on one foot'. These actions should only be followed if prefaced with the phrase 'Simon says'. Any players caught carrying out incorrect actions are eliminated. The winner is the last player who has successfully followed all the given commands. Play some appropriate music (Harry Potter is ideal) and give one fairy a 'freeze' wand and a wizard a 'defrost' wand and let the hocus pocus fun commence! Five minute stints of this game is certainly enough!

For a simple 'going home' present, buy little notepads and stick a label on the front of each one, saying 'POTIONS and SPELLS'. Fun feather pens and large sticks of colourful rock are also perfect party favours.

Abracadabra pin wheels

MAKES APPROX. 32 PIECES

These pastry delights are basically savoury palmiers and, despite appearances, take no time at all to make. What's more, they can be made several days before the party, kept in an airtight container and just reheated in a hot oven 20 minutes before serving. Cheese lovers are sure to appreciate an extra sprinkle of Cheddar over the pastries for the ultimate cheesy feast!

Preheat the oven to 200°C/gas mark 6 and line a baking tray with baking parchment.

Unroll the pastry with the longest edge closest to you and cut in half vertically.

Spread each half of the pastry with the tomato purée, followed by the grated Cheddar.

Lay the slices of ham across each half of the pastry.

Taking one half of the pastry at a time, roll the shortest edges over until they meet in the centre. Brush the bottom half with the beaten egg and flip the top half on top. Repeat this process with the other pastry half.

Carefully place on a baking tray, cover with clingfilm and put in the fridge to rest for 30 minutes.

Remove from the fridge, uncover and lightly brush both pastry rolls with beaten egg.

Using a sharp knife, or scissors, cut each pastry roll into 1cm slices. Arrange the slices on the baking tray, leaving plenty of space between each slice. Bake for 12–15 minutes or until golden.

Remove from the oven and serve warm.

you will need

- 320g ready-rolled puff pastry sheet
- 2 tablespoons tomato purée
- 100g Cheddar, finely grated
- 6 thin slices of honey-roasted ham
- 1 large egg, beaten

fairy bread

MAKES APPROX. 32 (DEPENDING ON COOKIE CUTTER SIZE)

This might be the easiest recipe in our book and may well be one of the most popular. Each little shape, covered in edible glitter and colourful sprinkles, looks magical and will disappear off the plate in a flash. They take seconds to put together but must be served straight away to avoid the bread going dry and curling up at the edges.

Spread a thin layer of butter on to one side of each of the pieces of bread. Using cookie cutters cut out a variety of shapes. We use wizards' hats, wands stars and fairy shapes.

Lay the shapes on a tray or dish with sides and cover with the sprinkles.

Place the sprinkle-covered shapes on a large plate and serve immediately.

you will need

800g white bread, thin or medium sliced

250g spreadable butter

80g hundreds and thousands or other sprinkles of your choice

pixie's potion

SERVES 8

You cannot go wrong with these cute mini chocolate cocktails, which are just perfect for any little pixie! These can be made and bottled up well ahead of the party, so you have one less thing to worry about. If you cannot find the vanilla syrup just use a teaspoon of vanilla extract instead.

Heat the milk in a pan over a low heat until warm and simmering.

Break the chocolate into pieces and add to the milk. Stir until completely melted, then remove from the heat.

Allow to cool completely before adding the vanilla syrup.

Pour the potion into a measuring jug or cocktail shaker and add the ice. Mix or shake well and then strain.

Pour into mini bottles, add the lids and place in the fridge to chill before serving.

For a bit of fun, stick a label onto each bottle with the children's names on.

you will need

300ml semi-skimmed milk

200g milk chocolate

80ml vanilla syrup (available at most large supermarkets) or 1 teaspoon vanilla extract

2 large handfuls of ice

wizard's cheesy cauldron

SERVES 8

This fun fondue is comfort food at its best. It is deliciously warming and fun to eat, so gather your wizards around the cauldron pot and watch their excited faces as they delve into this bubbling, cheesy concoction. Throw in some chunks of chorizo and mushrooms for the more adventurous kids.

Preheat the oven to 180°C/gas mark 4.

Take your bloomer or tin loaf and carefully chop off the lid – about 7.5cm in depth. To hollow out the loaf, gently cut round the sides – leaving about 2.5cm of dough on each side. Then slip your hands down the sides and loosen the dough on the base before removing the entire inside of the loaf in one go.

Using a sharp knife, chop the removed loaf into soldiers (about 2.5cm thick and about 10cm in length).

Place these soldiers or dippers onto a baking tray and put in the oven for about 5 minutes or until golden in colour. Remove from the oven and leave to cool.

In a large bowl, combine the crème fraîche, Cheddar, cooked pancetta, cooked spinach and tomato purée and beat together until combined.

Fill the empty loaf with the cheesy mixture before replacing the lid. Loosely wrap the loaf in some foil, place on a tray and bake in the oven for 45 minutes.

Remove from the oven and unwrap the foil and remove the lid. Place the loaf back in the oven for a further 10 minutes or until the cheesy mix is golden and bubbling.

Remove from the oven and leave to cool for 10 minutes, before placing on a basket along with the soldiers and let the wizards appreciate your culinary magic.

you will need

- 1 good-sized bloomer or tin loaf, brown or white
- 500ml crème fraîche
- 200g mild Cheddar, grated
- 200g pancetta, cooked and chopped
- 100g spinach, cooked, roughly chopped and well drained
- 1 tablespoon sun-dried tomato purée

Fairy Fritters

Flitter, fritter, flutter! Light, fluffy and yummy, these little savoury pancakes are a doddle to make. They have an incredible pick-upable quality for children and adults alike, so perhaps make extra if you have grown-ups coming too. The fritters can be made a day before the party and stored in an airtight container. Then simply add the toppings an hour before serving.

Sift the flour and baking powder in a bowl. Make a well in the middle and add the egg and gradually whisk in the milk to make a smooth batter. Stir in the sweetcorn.

Heat the oil in a large non-stick frying pan. Drop tablespoons of the batter in the pan, leaving gaps in between each fritter. Cook for 2 minutes, or until golden. Turn and repeat on the other side. Set the fritters aside.

In a mixing bowl, combine the avocado, cream cheese and lime juice and stir until smooth.

To serve, put a spoonful of avocado mousse onto the centre of each fritter, top with a few shards of crispy bacon and serve.

you will need

100g plain flour
1 tablespoon baking powder
1 large egg
150ml semi-skimmed milk
198g can sweetcorn, drained
1 tablespoon olive oil

for the avocado mousse

3 ripe avocados, peeled and de-stoned
80g cream cheese
2 teaspoons lime juice
40g crispy bacon, broken into shards, to serve

Fresh Fruity wands with popping candy

MAKES 10 ★

Our ethos of 'make food fun' cannot be truer than with these wands. Trying to get some children to touch fruit is not an easy task at the best of times but include a wand, some fresh berries and a jar of magic popping candy and you'll be holding back the hordes.

Thread the fruit onto a kebab skewer – first one strawberry, then the kiwi, pineapple, a grape and finish with two blueberries.

Place onto a plate with a jar of popping candy in the centre. (Do not remove the lid of the jar until you are ready to serve, otherwise the popping candy will lose its popping power!)

you will need

5 strawberries, halved

10 cubes of kiwi (approx. 3cm)

10 cubes of fresh pineapple (approx. 3cm)

10 large seedless red grapes (halved for small tots)

20 blueberries

150g popping candy

Hobgoblin's Gooey Brownies

MAKES 12 MINI BROWNIES

In folklore, a brownie resembles the mythological hob spirit, which is similar to a hobgoblin, so it was only appropriate that we included some of our chocolate brownies in this chapter. These little cubes of chocolate heaven are one of our bestsellers at Hats & Bells. The key is to remove the brownies from the oven when they are still slightly undercooked to ensure you achieve that irresistibly gooey texture.

Preheat the oven to 180°C/gas mark 4. Line a 20cm square or 20 x 24cm brownie tin with baking parchment and set aside.

Carefully melt the chocolate and butter together in a saucepan, over a low heat, stirring occasionally until smooth. Once melted, remove from the heat and leave to cool.

In a separate bowl, beat the eggs and sugar together until pale and fluffy using an electric whisk. This will take a few minutes, so be patient.

Add the chocolate mixture to the whisked eggs and sugar and beat until well combined.

Carefully add the flour to the mixture and stir well until smooth and fully incorporated.

Pour the mixture into the lined tin and bake for 15–20 minutes or until the top is dry but the middle is still soft. Be careful not to overbake – brownies need to be heavy and gooey inside.

Before serving, cut into mini cubes and dust with some sifted icing sugar. To finish, sprinkle with a few jelly beans or fresh berries, such as strawberries or blackberries.

you will need

190g good-quality dark chocolate (minimum 70 per cent cocoa solids)

190g salted butter

3 large eggs

150g golden caster sugar

115g plain flour

to decorate

icing sugar, for dusting

a handful of jelly beans or fresh berries

fairy Dust cupcakes

MAKES 24 MINI CUPCAKES AND 1 LARGE CUPCAKE ★

Without a doubt, the cupcake reigns supreme as king of any party and a tray or cake stand of cupcakes can make a great alternative to a birthday cake. More and more we are asked to make mini cupcakes – for these you will need a mini muffin tray and cases. We decorated ours with edible glitter and stars, but great fairy-themed candles and mini indoor sparklers are available to enhance the birthday singing and candle blowing experience (see Directory on page 204).

Preheat the oven to 180°C/gas mark 4. Line a 24-hole mini cupcake tray with mini paper cake cases and set aside. Place one stand-alone large cupcake case on a baking tray.

Cream the butter, sugar and vanilla extract together until pale and fluffy. Add the beaten eggs a little at a time, stirring the mixture continuously.

Fold in the flour and baking powder using a metal spoon. The mixture should drop off the spoon when it is ready; if it is a little stiff, add a couple of teaspoons of warm water and mix in.

Fill each cupcake case half-full with the mixture and bake for 10–12 minutes for the mini cakes and 12–15 minutes for the large one, or until golden brown.

Remove from the oven and leave to cool for 1 hour on a wire rack.

As these cakes are the birthday cake it is important to make them look as impressive as possible.

Using a piping bag and different textured and sized nozzles, you can create some great effects with the white butter icing before you add the sprinkles.

Sprinkle on mini edible stars, glitter and mini fondant wizard hats. To finish arrange the cakes onto a cupcake stand, and place a candle or indoor sparkler in the one large cupcake on the top of the stand to serve.

you will need

110g unsalted butter, softened

110g golden caster sugar

1 teaspoon vanilla extract

2 medium eggs, beaten

110g self-raising flour, sifted

1 teaspoon baking powder

500g White Butter Icing (see recipe page 17)

edible glitter, edible stars and other decorations of your choice

Knights and Princesses

Knights and Princesses

Without a doubt, this is one of the most popular themes for children's parties. Whether you are catering for boys, girls or a mix, there are endless ideas and decorative touches to keep your little ones amused and happy. If you are throwing a purely female party, then pink is the colour that every princess will be after but for an all-boy or mixed group, stick to gold, purple and red.

Find appropriately coloured tablecloths and runners for the 'banquet table' and laden it with plastic gold plates, cutlery, goblets and candlesticks, which can all be bought from online party shops. Lay generous bunches of grapes down the centre of the table, along with a good sprinkling of golden table confetti. Crowns should definitely feature on the party table, whether they be shop-bought or handmade. A great starter activity would be a crown decorating table, where children can customise their own crown masterpiece while everyone's arriving. If you are feeling really artistic, find some old sheets and depending on their size, cut them into 50cm strips. Using fabric paint or pens, draw some coats of arms onto the centre of each strip, before hanging them in the doorways and down the walls of the 'banqueting room'.

When your guests arrive at the party, ask a father with a strong, loud voice, or an entertainer if you have one, to introduce each knight or princess as he or she enters – for example, Princess Grace, Lord Sam, Lady Emily. Playing some medieval court music will help to set the scene and if you have an entertainer, why not ask him or her to dress as a court jester and entertain the children with juggling, stilt-walking and medieval magic? (Be sure to ask about such skills before you book the entertainer.) Wandering minstrels were a huge part of the royal courts, so why not split your royal guests into several groups and have them create and perform a short play or song? If you decide not to have an entertainer, designate a willing adult to oversee and help each group.

Try to serve as much of the food as possible on metallic (gold or silver) plates and in buckets. Using gold spray, paint pieces of A4 card, before writing down the menu on each one (in extra swirly, italic writing). Dot these menus down the table for your guests to read. Don't be afraid to serve both the sweet and the savoury food at the same time for this royal feast. In days of yore, it was all about luxurious chaos, so a table groaning with delectable treats (Henry VIII style) will wow your guests as well as be in keeping with how royal predecessors dined.

For 'going home' treats, think drawstring bags, juggling balls, knights and plastic horses and one of the party balloons. There is a lot of fun to be had at a Knights and Princesses party, so enjoy being creative.

palace pancetta pies

These are quite simply a tart without the pastry crust, so not even our yummy mummies need fear for their waistlines! There is nothing worse than stumbling across a quiche with a thick and stodgy pastry casing, so here we have simply baked the custard mixture in a pancetta coating, for a scrummy and crispy quiche alternative. Say goodbye to soggy bottoms forever!

Preheat the oven to 180°C/gas mark 4. Grease eight holes of a 12-hole muffin tin.

Line each muffin hole with three slices of pancetta. You might have to press and poke the pancetta a bit to get a perfect fit.

Whisk the eggs, cream, cheese, salt and basil leaves or chives together in a bowl until well combined and then divide the mixture equally among the eight pancetta cases.

Bake in the oven for 12–15 minutes or until the mixture is set and golden in colour.

Remove from the oven and leave to cool for 10 minutes before carefully removing from the tin. (A small palette knife can help remove any stubborn pies from the tin.)

Serve immediately or cold if preferred – both ways are delicious.

you will need

olive oil, for greasing

24 thin slices of pancetta

4 large eggs

200ml double cream

80g mild Cheddar or Gruyère, finely grated

pinch of salt

a small handful of freshly torn basil leaves or chopped chives

knights' and ladies' shield puffs

MAKES 8 ★

Every royal guest needs a proper banquet and it begins here with these easy puff-pastry shields. Be experimental and use different fish; we find that cod and hake work brilliantly too. These are best eaten freshly baked from the oven but do leave them to stand and cool for a few minutes, as they will be boiling-hot inside.

Preheat the oven to 180°C/gas mark 4. Line a baking tray with baking parchment.

Unroll the pastry and cut out 16 shield shapes with a cookie cutter (ours was approx. 8cm across) and eight mini stars.

Cut the salmon into small cubes and combine with the cream cheese and peas in a large bowl. Season with salt and freshly ground black pepper.

With a pastry brush, coat one side of eight of the shields with a light layer of beaten egg.

Place a heaped teaspoon of the salmon mixture onto the centre of eight of the pastry shields, leaving a 2mm gap around the edge with no filling.

Brush the egg mixture onto one side of the remaining pastry shields and place brushed-side down on top of each shield with the mixture, pressing the edges to seal the mini parcel.

Brush each of the top of the shields with egg and position the mini pastry stars in the middle. Make a small hole or slit in the top of the pastry so the steam can escape during baking.

Carefully place the shield puffs onto the lined baking tray and bake for 12–15 minutes or until the tops are golden brown.

Allow to cool for 5 minutes before serving.

you will need

320g ready-rolled puff pastry sheet

100g salmon fillet, skinned

80g cream cheese

40g peas, cooked and drained

salt and freshly ground black pepper

1 egg, beaten

golden wedges

SERVES 8–10

Quick, easy and filling, these sweet potato wedges make a great side dish and are a good alternative to your average, everyday chip. They can be cooked a few hours in advance and crisped up just before serving. Feel free to bake these wedges in different infused olive oils for extra flavour – basil, lemon and chilli (for the adults) are all delicious.

Preheat the oven to 200°C/gas mark 6. Lightly grease a large baking tray and set aside.

Put the sweet potatoes into a large bowl, drizzle with the oil and add the salt and poppy seeds. Mix well, using your hands, to ensure that all the potatoes are well coated.

Spread the wedges in a single layer over the baking tray and scatter over the thyme sprigs.

Bake for 35 minutes or until golden in colour and cooked through. (If you are cooking these ahead of time and plan to reheat the wedges in a hot oven before serving, then reduce this cooking time by 10 minutes.) Remove the thyme sprigs before assembling the wedges for serving.

To crisp up the wedges cooked ahead, preheat the oven to 220°C/gas mark 7 and spread out on a baking tray and cook for 10 minutes.

For a bit of fun, line three or four large, wide-brimmed tumblers or mini vases with baking parchment and fill each one generously with the wedges. Serve with little ramekins of ketchup and/or mayonnaise on the side if you wish.

you will need

olive or vegetable oil, for greasing and drizzling

900g sweet potatoes, peeled and chopped into thick wedges

1 teaspoon salt flakes

2 teaspoons poppy seeds

5 sprigs of fresh thyme

tomato ketchup or mayonnaise, to serve (optional)

strawberry Biscuit towers

MAKES 8

This is one of the very first recipes we ever made as 11-year-old schoolgirls. The triple-stacked towers have a tangy cream to sandwich them together. We like to use passion fruit pulp, but lemon curd works just as well and both will give these biscuit towers a real kick and zing.

Preheat the oven to 180°C/gas mark 4. Line two baking trays with baking parchment and set aside.

Sift the flour, salt and cornflour into a mixing bowl and stir together. Add the butter and using your fingertips, rub the butter into the flour until it resembles fine breadcrumbs. Then stir in the sugar.

In a separate bowl, lightly beat together the egg and vanilla extract, before pouring into the buttery mixture and combining with a round ended knife or fork.

Now, using your hands, gently form the mixture into a ball. Cover with clingfilm and place in the fridge to rest for 30 minutes.

Next, unwrap the dough and place onto a lightly floured surface. Using a rolling pin, roll it out until about 5mm thick. Using a crown-shaped cookie cutter (approx. 6cm across), stamp out the biscuit shapes. Knead the remaining dough together and re-roll to cut more biscuits. Repeat until you have 24 crowns.

Place the biscuits on the prepared baking trays and bake for 15 minutes or until golden in colour. Leave on the baking trays to firm up for a few minutes, then carefully transfer the biscuits onto a wire rack to cool completely.

Meanwhile, gently fold three quarters of the passion fruit pulp or lemon curd into the whipped cream. (Do not overmix – it is nice to be able to see a ripple of colour in the cream.)

Place a teaspoon of the mixture and a couple of strawberry slices on top of eight of the crowns. Stack another crown on top and repeat the process until you have a stack of three. To serve, dust with icing sugar and sprinkle with the remaining passion fruit pulp and some gold leaf.

you will need

200g self-raising flour, plus extra for dusting

pinch of salt

25g cornflour

100g salted butter, cubed

100g golden caster sugar

1 egg, lightly beaten

4 drops of vanilla extract

pulp of 3 passion fruits or 2 heaped tablespoons of lemon curd

150ml double cream, lightly whipped

16 good-sized strawberries, hulled and sliced

icing sugar, for dusting

gold leaf, for decoration

Glittery Gem cake Pops

MAKES 46

Cake pops have become massively popular at parties, simply because they have both the wow factor and taste fabulous. We have had great fun making a huge variety of cake pops for all sorts of occasions. If you don't have a cake pop stand a block of oasis or foam works just as well.

In a large mixing bowl, crumble the sponge with your fingers until it is the consistency of breadcrumbs.

Add the Chocolate Butter Icing a dessertspoon at a time and mix with the sponge cake crumbs. You may not need all the icing – your mixture is ready when you can roll it into a ball that is fudge-like in consistency and there are no crumbs. If you use too much icing the mixture will be soggy and too heavy to stay on the sticks.

Take a small amount of the mixture in your hands, about the size of a ping-pong ball, and roll it into a ball shape. Place the balls onto a non-stick baking tray and chill in the fridge for 2 hours.

Melt the white chocolate or candy melts in a heatproof bowl fitted over a pan of barely simmering water, making sure the bowl doesn't touch the water. Dip one end of the cake pop sticks into the melted chocolate or candy melts and then push halfway into the centre of one of the balls of cake.

Pick up the cake, holding the stick, and dip into the melted chocolate (or candy melts) until the whole ball is covered. Hold it over the bowl until it isn't dripping and then place in the cake pop stand or in a block of oasis covered in foil. Sprinkle the cake pop with your chosen edible glitter or sprinkles and leave to set. Repeat this process with half of the balls of cake.

Now, melt the dark chocolate or candy melts in a heatproof bowl fitted over a pan of barely simmering water, making sure the bowl doesn't touch the water. Repeat the coating steps above with the remaining balls of cake.

Leave the cake pops in a stand in a cool place (not the fridge or they will discolour) for at least 4 hours.

you will need

- 1 x 20cm round White Chocolate Vanilla Sponge Cake (see recipe on page 16)
- 250g Chocolate Butter Icing (made using half the quantities in the recipe on page 17)
- 250g white chocolate or coloured candy melts
- 250g dark chocolate (minimum 70 per cent cocoa solids) or coloured candy melts
- edible glitter and sprinkles, to decorate

knight and princess castle cake

SERVES 15–20

This may seem like an ambitious cake and we won't say that it is super easy, but the extra time you spend making it will be worth all the effort. Other ideas for this theme include: a shield, a crown or making this cake in grey icing to become a fort.

Place the round cake on the centre of a 45cm round cake board. You can cover this in light green fondant icing if you wish. Cover the cake in a thin layer of white butter icing to contain all the crumbs and create a smooth base for the fondant icing.

Using cookie cutters, cut out twelve 7.5cm circles of sponge and two 8.5cm circles of sponge from the rectangular cakes. Sandwich together three of the 7cm circles using butter icing between each one. Repeat this with the remaining circles until you have your four towers. Sandwich together the 8.5cm pieces of cake with butter icing, which will make the central turret.

Roll out 500g of light pink fondant icing on a lightly floured surface into a circle large enough to cover the cake and to approx. 1cm thick. Place over the cake, trim to fit and smooth with lightly sugared hands.

Wrap a brick or stone impression mat (which can be bought online or from a craft store) around the cake and rub gently to create a brick effect. If you do not have an impression mat you can use a knife to create a brick pattern on the icing.

Roll out 800g of light pink fondant icing on a lightly floured surface until it is approx. 5mm thick and slightly taller than the towers. Cover each tower with a thin layer of butter icing, which will act as the glue. Wrap each tower in the pink fondant icing.

Cover the 8.5cm turret with a thin layer of butter icing and cover with the light pink fondant icing.

you will need

- 1 x 20cm round White Chocolate Vanilla Sponge Cake (see recipe on page 16 but use half the quantity of ingredients and cook for 20 minutes)
- 150g light green ready-made fondant icing (optional)
- 500g White Butter Icing (see recipe page 16)
- 2 x 25 x 34cm rectangular White Chocolate Vanilla Sponge Cakes (see recipe on page 16)
- icing sugar, for dusting
- 1.5kg light pink ready-made fondant icing
- 25g brown ready-made fondant icing
- 100ml Apricot Glaze (see recipe on page 17)
- 500g light blue ready-made fondant icing
- 200g light blue butter icing
- 1 white icing pen

Lay the impression mat on a table and roll the towers and the turret gently over it. Don't worry if the indents are not consistent.

Place each tower on the cake board on each 'corner' of the cake, using a blob of butter icing to stick them down with the icing seam facing towards the cake. Stick the turret to the centre of the round cake using butter icing as the glue.

Roll out the brown fondant icing on a lightly floured surface until it is approx. 5mm thick. Cut out four 5 x 2cm rectangles, six 3.5 x 2cm rectangles and four 2 x 1.5cm rectangles. These are the windows. Then cut one 5 x 4.5cm rectangle for the door to the castle. On one side of all the windows brush a thin layer of apricot glaze and stick the large windows on the outside of the towers, the medium windows on the main castle circle and the small window on the top turret. Stick the door on one side of the main part of the castle.

Take the light blue fondant icing and divide it into four equal-sized pieces. With lightly sugared hands roll them into cone shapes. Using some of the white butter icing, stick the cones on the top of the towers.

Place the blue butter icing in a piping bag with a small star nozzle. Pipe around the base of the cones sat on top of the towers and around the central turret to finish the edges off neatly.

Using a white icing pen, put a cross on each window and a door handle on the door.

Finally finish off the castle by making small rectangles of pink fondant icing using the remaining icing. Use a little blob from the icing pen to stick these on top of the castle around the edge of the main cake.

Royal Fruit Buckets

MAKES APPROX. 50 PIECES ★

Eating fruit never tasted so good! These little fruity buckets are simple and quick to make and adored by children. To give variety of colour, we often use both white and dark chocolate, or even go glorious technicolour and dip the fruit in coloured sugar or sugar sprinkles. These can be made ahead of time but must be kept in a cool room to avoid any melting disasters, especially in the summer.

Line a tray or baking tray with baking parchment.

Melt the chocolate in a heatproof bowl fitted over a pan of barely simmering water, making sure the bowl doesn't touch the water.

Place a toothpick into one end of a grape and dip into the melted chocolate and set aside on the lined tray. Repeat this process with the remaining grapes.

Hold each strawberry by the green hull and dip into the melted chocolate and set aside on the lined tray.

Place the chocolate-covered fruit in a cool place for a couple of hours. You can put it in the fridge but the chocolate will lose its shine.

To serve, pile up in mini buckets or flowerpots to serve.

you will need

300g dark chocolate (minimum 70 per cent cocoa solids)
400g seedless green grapes
400g strawberries

Land of Milk and Honey

SERVES 12

Milk and cookies never tasted or looked so good! The milk bottles and crates are easy to find online and will be a real talking point long after your royal guests have left. This is a great one to prepare in advance – the milk can be made up to 24 hours before the party and left to chill in the fridge and the cookies keep for up to five days if stored in an airtight container. The lavender adds an unusual twist and, surprisingly, kids seem to love it.

To make the cookies, preheat the oven to 190°C/gas mark 5. Line a baking tray with baking parchment and set aside.

Beat together the sugar, butter, vanilla extract and honey until pale and fluffy. Stir in the flour and lavender until combined and a dough is formed. Wrap the dough in clingfilm and leave to rest in the fridge for 30 minutes.

On a lightly floured surface, roll the dough to a thickness of 5mm.

Using a star-shaped cutter (approx. 7cm across), cut out 24 shortbread stars. Using the end of a straw, puncture a hole in the centre of each biscuit before placing on a baking tray. Bake for 10–12 minutes until firm and golden.

Remove from the oven and using the straw again, quickly repuncture any holes which might have closed up during the cooking process. Leave to cool for 5 minutes, before transferring onto a wire rack.

To make the milk, split the milk into two measuring jugs. Add 2 teaspoons of food colouring to each jug and stir to colour the milk. Pour the milk into 12 bottles or glasses and chill in the fridge.

Just before serving, put a straw in each of the bottles and thread two shortbread stars onto each straw and balance on the top of each milk bottle or glass.

For the cookies

55g golden caster sugar

125g salted butter, softened

1 teaspoon vanilla extract

1 tablespoon set (not clear) honey

180g plain flour, sifted, plus extra for dusting

1 teaspoon dried lavender buds

For the milk

1.2 litres semi-skimmed milk

2 teaspoons pink food colouring

2 teaspoons blue food colouring

UNDER THE SEA

UNDER THE SEA

The world is your oyster with this theme and it is appropriate for any age group. Depending on whether you have more boys or more girls, you might want to steer it more towards pirates or mermaids. (Don't forget, girls love being pirates too!)

Have fun from the start by making invitations. Use green paper invites, zipped into clear sandwich bags and sprinkle glitter and sand inside or make your own treasure map invitations and write the details onto burnt brown paper, scrolled up with red ribbon. Involve the birthday girl or boy here too and indulge your inner artist.

To set the scene, make sure you have a good soundtrack playing: Disney's *The Little Mermaid* and *The Pirates of the Caribbean* will certainly get everyone in the mood. We find this is such an easy theme to work with and no matter how big or small your budget, there are bucketloads of ideas to suit every pocket. For a simple and effective decoration, fill different-sized glass vases with pretty shells and sand and dot little plastic buckets and spades around the party room for a real 'beachy' feel. We think a giant fishing net looks fabulous on any party table, especially when scattered with more shells, fake starfish and emptied and cleaned crab shells. If having a few goldfish in bowls on your table sounds a bit far-fetched, why not fill bowls with

cheesy goldfish crackers that the children can help themselves to, perhaps even using mini fishing nets? Hang metallic green, blue and silver streamers from your doors and windows and fill your room with floating tropical fish balloons (though plain blue and green balloons work fine too). Fill old wine bottles with personal messages for your guests and hide them around the party room or garden for them to find on arrival. At each place name, leave pirate eye patches and fortune-telling fish, both of which can be picked up very cheaply from all good party shops or online.

How about a Lucky Dip? Fill an old chest or large ice bucket with metallic streamers and shiny silver paper and fill with appropriate goodies for your guests. Think fake pearl necklaces, fish bath toys, themed key rings, pirate bandanas and sea life pop-ups. Depending on your guests, you might want to consider colour coding the boys and girls presents to avoid any embarrassment or disappointment!

If the weather is fine, you could have some of the party al fresco. Set up a game of 'Catch a Starfish' – you'll need a small paddling pool, eight rubber starfish and a small fishing net. Float the starfish on the water and ask each guest to catch four or more starfish in 30 seconds, to win a prize. (Adults must catch all eight!)

For a slightly more energetic game, give what we call 'Blast the Cannon Ball' a go. Tie an inflated black balloon to each of your guests' legs before they all try to pop one another's balloon, while all the time protecting their own. The last one with a balloon still intact, is the winner. (Make sure you have a referee on hand as, in our experience, this game can get quite competitive!)

Keep 'going home' gifts simple – for instance, little bags filled with chocolate gold coins and a helium balloon (from the party space), will keep your guests more than happy.

floundering fish cones

SERVES 8

This dish is on the menu at 99 per cent of the parties we cater for. Every morsel is demolished and even the parents try to get their hands on this all-time favourite. Cod, haddock and hake all work well – and it's often a good plan to double the quantities, as these will swim off the plates!

In a large bowl, mix together the breadcrumbs, Ritz biscuits and Parmesan and set aside.

Take the fish strips and lightly roll them in the flour, before dipping them in the beaten egg, followed by the breadcrumb mix. Repeat this process, until all the goujons are fully coated.

Heat some oil in a large frying pan and add the goujons, about six at a time. Fry on all sides for 2 minutes or until golden brown and cooked through.

Serve immediately or leave in a warm oven until needed.

Make little cones from wrapping paper or newspaper or buy mini bamboo cones. To serve, prop them up in flowerpots or cone holders (which you can find easily online).

you will need

150g fresh white breadcrumbs

150g Ritz biscuits, finely crushed

60g Parmesan, finely grated

900g skinless cod fillets (or other white fish), cut into 1cm thick strips

2 heaped tablespoons plain flour

1 large egg, beaten

olive oil, for frying

vegetable sea dome

Parents normally feel there should be a 'healthy' option on a party table and this dome, which looks fabulous as a table centrepiece, ticks all the boxes. We have witnessed children who don't usually eat vegetables snapping these up and, of course, when one child starts, the rest tend to follow.

Cut the watermelon in half and place flat-side down on a tray, chopping board or large flat plate.

Cut the cheese into 2cm slices and then stamp out the star shapes using a mini star cookie cutter (ours was about 1.5 cm across). Set aside. The leftover cheese can be used in the Baguette Boats (see page 100).

Cut the cucumber into 2cm thick slices.

Take a kebab skewer and pierce a slice of cucumber and then a cherry tomato and finally a cheese star. Repeat the process. Once you have used up all the cheese, cucumber and tomato pierce the skewers into the watermelon and take to the table to serve.

you will need

1 large watermelon
400g Cheddar or Red Leicester
2 cucumbers
30 cherry tomatoes

Baguette Boats

SERVES 6

These very simple hot sandwiches are original and truly scrumptious. You can add anything to these boats – ham, salami, cooked chicken, tuna mayonnaise, cherry tomatoes, pitted baby black olives, strands of roasted peppers, sweetcorn and cheese, cheese and even more...cheese! Have fun playing around with different flavours.

Preheat the oven to 180°C/gas mark 4.

Cut the baguette in half lengthways, so the top and bottom are separated. Remove the majority of the dough so you have two hollow boat shapes. (You could make croutons with any of the leftover dough and dunk these into the cheesy boats, once cooked.)

Brush a thin layer of olive oil and pesto onto the inside surfaces of the baguettes.

In a large bowl, lightly mix together the grated mozzarella, ham, tomatoes, mayonnaise and fresh basil (and any additional ingredients you might like; you might need a few more dollops of mayonnaise to combine the extra ingredients).

Pile the cheesy mix on top of each half of the baguette and place in the oven for 15–20 minutes or until melting and warm.

For a nautical edge, cut pieces of card into triangles and thread them onto cocktail sticks to make sails for the baguette boats. These look best as big boats so you may need a few 'sails' or one large one.

you will need

- 1 large baguette
- 2 teaspoons olive oil
- 3 tablespoons red or green pesto
- 100g mozzarella, grated
- 100g cooked ham or gammon, cut into chunks
- 100g cherry tomatoes, halved
- 1 heaped tablespoon mayonnaise
- a handful of fresh basil, torn

mermaid shell meringues

MAKES 10–12 SHELL SANDWICHES ✦

Hatty's mother is the queen of meringues and she has taught us how to make crocodiles, rabbits, swans and snakes. Fear not, we're keeping these meringues simple – similar to the shape of seashells. Make the meringues in advance, as they will keep for ages if stored in an airtight container. However you will need to make the cream filling and decorate them fairly last minute.

Preheat oven to 120°C/gas mark ½. Line a baking tray with baking parchment and set aside.

Whisk the egg whites in a clean, dry bowl until they are stiff. Add half the sugar and whisk until the mixture forms stiff peaks.

Fold the rest of the sugar into the mixture until combined and the mixture is shiny and stiff.

Add a couple of drops of food colouring and fold into the mixture but do not completely combine, as you want a slightly rippled effect.

Transfer the mixture into a piping bag with a star nozzle and use this to put small circles of mixture onto the baking parchment, leaving gaps in between. (You can also use a teaspoon for this if you don't have a piping bag.) If you want to be very precise, mark out some circles on the baking parchment, turn it over, so that the pen mark doesn't seep onto the meringue, and then pipe using your circle template.

Bake for about 1½ hours or until the meringues lift easily off the baking parchment. Carefully transfer the meringues to a wire rack to cool.

Whisk the double cream and golden caster sugar together until light and fluffy.

Using a teaspoon of cream, sandwich two meringues together, before scattering a few silver balls over the cream. Repeat with the remaining meringues.

you will need

2 medium egg whites

125g caster sugar

food colouring (pink, purple, blue or green)

for the filling

150ml double cream

10g golden caster sugar

30g silver balls

Pirate Jack Gingersnaps

MAKES 10

Well, 'shiver me timbers' – these are the best ginger biscuits ever! Plus, you can customise the recipe with a handful of oats (to give these snaps a little texture), or mix and match the spices according to your child's taste buds. You can serve these warm from the oven or go for full-on decorated versions.

Preheat the oven to 180°C/gas mark 4. Line a baking tray with baking parchment and set aside.

Cream together the butter and sugar until pale and light; this will take a few minutes, so be patient.

Beat in the egg and syrup before sifting in the flour, cinnamon and ginger. Fold the mixture together until smooth and fully combined. Spoon small, equal-sized balls onto the prepared tray, then flatten each one slightly using the back of a fork.

Bake the biscuits in the oven for about 15 minutes or until golden. Leave to cool completely before decorating.

Dust the work surface with icing sugar and roll out the pale pink fondant icing until 1cm in thickness. Using a round cutter (that of a similar size to your baked biscuits), stamp out 10 discs (the pirates' faces). Brush a little water on the back of each circle and place on top of each biscuit.

Repeat the process with the red icing but stamp out only five discs. Using a sharp knife, cut these discs in half and again dab a little water on the back of each one before placing over the top of the pink icing – these are the pirates' hats.

Decorate the hats with different coloured Smarties or other small coloured chocolates, before drawing on eyes, moustaches, patches (or whatever else takes your fancy) on the pink icing with the black icing pen.

The icing will take a few hours to dry, so leave somewhere cool before storing in an airtight container, where they will happily keep for 2–3 days.

you will need

125g unsalted butter, softened
125g dark brown soft sugar
1 medium egg, beaten
2 tablespoons golden syrup
190g self-raising flour
$1/2$ teaspoon ground cinnamon
1 teaspoon ground ginger

for the decoration

icing sugar, for dusting
125g pale pink ready-made fondant icing
125g red ready-made fondant icing
Smarties or other small coloured chocolates
1 black icing pen

scallywags' slushy punch

Ahoy there! Landlubbers and buccaneers alike will find that this grog puts hairs on chests! Deliciously refreshing and oh-so popular and for the adults, you can always add a tot (or two) of rum.

Pour all the liquids into a 2.5 litre jug.

Put a handful of crushed ice into eight hollow coconuts or glasses.

Fill each coconut or glass with the punch. Serve immediately with a straw and paper umbrella if you wish.

you will need

1 litre lemonade
500ml ginger beer
250ml apple juice
250ml pineapple juice
crushed ice

treasure map cake

With this cake you can easily combine the pirate and mermaid themes. You really can make it as simple or as complicated as you like, by adding palm trees, seashells, pirate figures, a treasure chest with coins and even a mermaid or two in the sea. Other cake ideas for this theme include a pirate's face, pirate hook, parrot, 2D or 3D mermaid or an under the sea scene.

Sandwich the cakes together using approx. 2 tablespoons of the butter icing. Carefully centre the cake on a 30.5cm round cake board.

Using a sharp knife, cut a small circular hole (approx. 4cm in diameter) in the top of the cake somewhere towards the centre and carefully spoon out the cake.

Place some 'treasure' in the hole – a handful of small sweets is perfect (be sure to take any wrappers off).

Carefully slice the top off the piece of cake you cut out and use it to cover the hole.

Place a toothpick in the top of the treasure spot, so you can remember roughly where it is and can later mark the spot with an 'X'.

Place the remaining butter icing in a bowl and tint it blue, with a few drops of food colouring.

Cover the cake in approx. one third of the blue butter icing, creating a thin and smooth layer to contain all the crumbs.

Using the remaining blue butter icing, spatula another layer of blue butter icing over the cake, but don't worry about it being completely smooth as this is the sea.

you will need

2 x 25 x 34cm rectangular White Chocolate Vanilla Sponge Cakes (see recipe page 16)

750g White Butter Icing (see recipe page 17)

a handful of Smarties or other small coloured chocolates, or other small sweets

blue food colouring

100g yellow ready-made fondant icing

1 black icing pen (optional)

100g gold chocolate coins

Lay the yellow fondant icing on a smooth work surface dusted with icing sugar. Roll the icing out, until it is approx. 1cm thick and cut into an island shape. Place on the centre of the cake.

Now that you have your sea and your island, you can decorate as much as you like. For a simple decoration, use a black icing pen to make an 'X' where the treasure is buried and then make a dotted line leading from the 'X' around the island and ending at the shoreline.

Other things you can scatter on the island can be made from fondant icing (in 2D or 3D and don't worry about scale, it's more exciting if everything is different) include a treasure chest, palm trees, mermaids in the sea, Jolly Roger flag and a compass (as simple as a cross with North, East, South, West marked on it).

Scatter gold coins around the base of the cake board and serve.

HMS Jellies

MAKES 40 BOATS ⭐

Jellies that don't need spoons! All your party guests will love these colourful 'boat' jellies. Pop flags in each one, with the children's names on and watch as they're swiped from the plate, faster than a gunpowder fuse. If you've got time, you can create stripy jellies by filling the 'boats' half full and leaving them to set in the fridge, before pouring in another colour.

Cut the oranges in half crosswise and hollow out, leaving the 'cup' of rind.

Prepare the five jelly flavours according to the packet instructions.

Fill the orange halves with each flavour and place the halves in a deep muffin tin. There may well be leftover jelly (depending on the size of the oranges), which you can either use to make extra boats or pour into a food container and refrigerate for later use.

Put the jellies in the fridge to set for 5 hours.

Remove the jellies from the fridge and cut each half into two using a sharp knife.

Place a flag in each wedge (40 in total) and place them in rainbow colour order on a large chopping board or flat plate to serve.

you will need

10 small oranges
135g packet strawberry jelly
135g packet orange jelly
135g packet lemon jelly
135g packet lime jelly
135g packet blackcurrant jelly

SPACE AND STAR ODYSSEY

SPACE AND STAR ODYSSEY

If your child is a budding astronaut in the making, then why not throw them a Space and Star Odyssey party? A very popular theme for many years and there is certainly no shortage of ideas for decoration and games, however old or new. Foil will be your new best friend, so make sure you have plenty in your kitchen drawer!

To set the scene (make sure you draw the curtains/blinds when party time comes), cover tables with black tablecloths, cups and plates and use long strips of tin foil as table runners. Sprinkle over multicoloured star-shaped confetti and run a string of battery powered fairy lights down the centre of the table. As with any party, you can really go to town but make sure you stick to your budget and available time, otherwise your enthusiasm may run past its limit.

Hang a 3D Solar System from the ceiling (these can be bought as a set online or made from papier mâché if you want a craft project in the weeks beforehand) or buy or make some coloured star decorations for hanging. Foil curtains for doorways can be sourced online or if you fancy – seeing as foil is your new best friend – you could fashion a DIY version. If you can make the room dark enough, then there are plenty of glow-in-the-dark stickers and decorations you could source.

Balloons can add instant impact, so look into having a mix of black, silver and purple, with star weights attached to the ribbon for any helium versions. Foil stars, astronauts and aliens would really help to create the right mood, so if your budget allows it, perhaps get a handful of these. If you have time, make foil-covered shaped name badges for each of your guests and for example, refer to them as Commander David or Pilot Chloe.

For extra decorative flourishes, you can fill

silver bowls with flying saucer sweets, popping candy in sachets and rest little chocolate foil planes on beds of marshmallows (these look better if displayed in a clear mixing bowl or vase). Be sure to place party poppers (ideal for children over five years old) and tubes of bubbles at each name setting and stick sparklers into foil-covered watermelons, ready for the children to light after they have finished their tea (do make sure there are a few adults to supervise the sparklers). If you decide to make the rocket birthday cake, source some fountain candles, as these will give a fantastic illusion that the cake is about to take off.

If the sun is shining, then take advantage! Outside games, such as frisbee and a water balloon fight are great ways of building up your astronauts' appetites. Solar Seek is another popular game, which can be undertaken inside or out. Roll up several balls of tin foil to create planets (each ball should be golf ball size). Create at least three planets for every guest that will be taking part. Hide the planets throughout the party area before splitting your guests into teams of three, providing each with a small bag or basket. On 'go', the children have 5 minutes to find as many planets as possible and the team who collect the most, are the winners. Other house-friendly options to consider are Tag in the Dark, (using glow sticks) or the ever popular Smartie Game (or as we like to call it Sucking Planets). Pour several tubes of Smarties onto a large tray and give each of your

astronauts a paper cup and a straw. On 'take off', they have to suck up as many Smarties as they can in one minute, sucking on their straw and without using their hands. The person with the most Smarties in his/her cup is the winner. If you live in a non-residential area, why not give each of your guests a paper lantern to send into space. Attach little luggage labels to each lantern and before lighting them, let each child write a message before making a wish as they let them go. This is always a special and memorable way to end any party.

Why not fill see-through bags with bouncy balls, spinning tops, space-themed stickers, flying saucer sweets, along with a generous sprinkling of edible glitter. Or go with the foil flow and make silver parcels of 'going home' treats sealed with cosmic stickers.

shooting burger planets

Mini shaped burgers are a perfect finger food for any party and this is an original spin on serving an old classic. For a full-on shooting star effect, you could cover flowerpots or vases with lots of foil, both inside and out, and stand the burger sticks upright in the pots.

Preheat the oven to 130°C/gas mark 1.

Heat a little oil in a large non-stick frying pan and gently fry the onion over a medium heat until softened.

Combine the onion with the mince, egg, herbs and tomato ketchup in a mixing bowl and blend together using your fingers.

Split the mixture into eight equal parts and roll each portion between your hands to form small burgers.

Add a little oil to the frying pan and fry the burgers for 2 minutes on each side, or until cooked through.

Put the burgers on a baking tray, cover in foil and put in the oven to keep warm.

Using a star-shaped cookie cutter, cut out stars from the burger buns.

Remove the burgers from the oven. Thread the ingredients onto eight kebab skewers. We like the following order of ingredients but feel free to mix it up – cherry tomato, top of the burger roll, burger patty, cheese, bottom of the burger roll, cherry tomato.

Serve the burger sticks standing up in a flowerpot or vase.

you will need

vegetable or olive oil, for frying
$1/2$ onion, finely chopped
400g lean beef mince
1 large egg, beaten
1 teaspoon dried mixed herbs
2 tablespoons tomato ketchup
8 burger buns, buttered
16 cherry tomatoes
8 thick slices of Red Leicester

mini sputnik spuds

MAKES 20

Astronauts are curious about other worlds and little astronauts can be curious about new foods, so include something a little different in your party menu in the shape of these Sputnik Spuds. Use the best quality pancetta you can afford, as it really does make all the difference.

Preheat the oven to 200°C/gas mark 6 and grease a medium-sized roasting tray with a little oil.

Put the baby new potatoes into a saucepan, cover with cold water, add the salt and gently bring to the boil.

Once the water is boiling, cook the potatoes for about 5–6 minutes or until you can stick a fork into them without too much resistance. (You do not want your potatoes to be falling apart when prodded.) Once cooked, take the potatoes off the heat and drain well.

Put the potatoes into a large bowl, sprinkle over the oregano and set aside to cool.

When the potatoes are cool enough to handle, carefully wrap a piece of pancetta around each one, securing it with a toothpick.

Put the Sputnik Spuds onto the greased baking tray and bake for 30 minutes, turning them over halfway through cooking, or until the pancetta is crispy and dark. Remove from the oven.

Leave the potatoes to cool for 5 minutes, while you pour the sour cream into a ramekin or small bowl, adding the chopped chives.

To serve, pile the potatoes high on a small plate, alongside the sour cream and chive dip.

you will need

vegetable oil, for greasing
20 baby new potatoes (the large ones are best as they shrink)
pinch of salt
1 teaspoon dried oregano
20 thin strips of pancetta

to serve

150ml sour cream
1 small bunch of chives, chopped

martians' fingers

These were Annabel's favourite party food when she was little, so wc couldn't not share them with you! Forget frozen and fast food chicken nuggets – these are in another league. For an adult version, add a good shake of paprika or cracked black pepper to the chicken, before frying.

Place the chicken goujons into a bowl and sprinkle over a little salt and the chopped tarragon, if using.

Pour over the buttermilk and using your hands, mix together, ensuring all the chicken is finely coated.

Cover the chicken mix with clingfilm and leave in the fridge to tenderise for at least 24 hours.

When you are ready to cook the goujons, put the cornflakes or pretzels into a food processor and pulse for a few seconds until they have broken down into large crumbs. If you don't have a food processor, put the cornflakes or pretzels in a large food bag and bash them with a rolling pin. (Do not over-pulse/bash – you want good sized crumbs not sawdust!) Pour the crumbs into a medium-sized bowl.

Remove the chicken goujons from the fridge and gently shake off any excess buttermilk before dipping each one into the crumbs, coating each piece fully and setting aside on a plate. Repeat this dipping until all goujons are coated.

Heat a little oil in a large frying pan and when the oil begins to sizzle, add your goujons (five or six at a time). Cook each piece for about 3 minutes on each side or until golden and cooked through. Remove the cooked goujons from the frying pan and cover with foil to keep warm. Repeat this process with the remaining goujons.

Once all the goujons have been cooked, drain them on a plate lined with kitchen paper, before serving in mini paper cones or buckets, with little pots of ketchup and mayonnaise.

you will need

450g chicken breasts, skinned and cut into chunky goujons (fingers)

pinch of salt

1 teaspoon finely chopped fresh tarragon, (optional)

200ml buttermilk

150g cornflakes or pretzels

olive oil, for frying

ketchup and mayonnaise, to serve

asteroid belt cookies

You can make cookies in many shapes and colours but using food colouring in cookie dough produces rather too vibrant a result for us. So, we've experimented and have found that the ultimate trick for a super colour-dusting is to add coloured sprinkles or sugar strands to the mix.

Preheat the oven to 180°C/gas mark 4. Line two large baking trays with baking parchment.

In a large mixing bowl, mix the butter and sugar together with an electric mixer or wooden spoon, until combined.

Add the egg to the mixture and beat until light and fluffy.

Stir in the flour and the bicarbonate of soda and beat together. Add the sprinkles and mix well.

Make walnut-sized balls of the mixture and place them on the baking trays with plenty of space in between as they will spread out when cooking.

Bake the cookies for 12 minutes or until golden.

Remove from the oven and leave to harden on the baking trays for 10 minutes and then carefully transfer to a wire rack to cool.

Pile the cookies into a tower on a serving plate.

you will need

- 110g salted butter
- 160g soft brown sugar
- 1 medium egg
- 175g plain flour, sifted
- ½ teaspoon bicarbonate of soda
- 100g coloured sprinkles (avoid pastel colours)

explosive mars meteors

Popping candy – the exploding ingredient in this recipe – is more readily available these days and who can resist adding it to a party recipe as a surprise? These chocolate biscuity treats not only taste divine but are also fun to make. They can be made a few days before and stored in an airtight container.

Line a non-stick 20cm square or 20 x 24cm brownie tin with baking parchment and set aside.

In a large bowl, use your hands to crush the digestive biscuits into medium-sized pieces (not too small). Set aside.

In a medium saucepan, melt the butter, chocolate and syrup over a low heat, stirring occasionally, ensuring the mixture does not burn. Once melted, remove from the heat and leave to cool for 5 minutes.

Once the mixture has cooled, add the crushed biscuits, honeycomb, marshmallows and popping candy and gently mix together until everything is coated.

Pour the chocolate mixture into the lined tin and transfer to the fridge for 4 hours or until set.

Once set, remove from the fridge and lift out of the tray, pulling up the edges of the baking parchment.

Leave in a cool place for 5 minutes to soften, then take a round cookie cutter (ours was 5cm across), and stamp out discs and set aside. Repeat this process until you have used up all of the cake.

Next, place the Mars bar pieces into a small saucepan and gently melt over a low heat, stirring frequently.

Once smooth and melted, remove from the heat and spread a thin layer of the melted chocolate on top of all the space discs.

For the decorations, make coils from the strawberry bootlaces and stick them onto the centre of each galactic disc, before adding the decorations of your choice.

you will need

300g digestive biscuits

250g unsalted butter

400g dark chocolate (minimum 70 per cent cocoa solids)

3 tablespoons golden syrup

160g honeycomb, crushed

100g mini marshmallows

50g popping candy

3 x 58g Mars bars, chopped into small pieces

to decorate

strawberry bootlaces

jelly beans

white chocolate buttons, halved

1 small jar of hundreds and thousands

1 small jar of chocolate stars

cosmic cones

Well, this is one way to eat part of your five-a-day! Positively naughty food starts right here, with a serious bang. Stuff these cones full with your child's favourite ingredients or better still, allow them to make their own. If the weather is nice, encourage your little guests to eat these outside, to save your clean carpets from death by chocolate.

Preheat the oven to 180°C/gas mark 4.

Layer up the ingredients inside the waffle cones. You can play with the order but we've found the best combination to be: 1.5cm banana pushed gently into the bottom of the cone, 10g chocolate, one marshmallow, 5g chocolate and then a further two marshmallows. Repeat this for all the cones.

Wrap the cones individually in foil and place on the baking tray and bake for 15 minutes.

Unwrap the cones, leaving foil around the bottoms, and hand one to each child.

you will need

8 waffle ice cream cones

120g milk chocolate, broken into pieces

24 marshmallows

1 large or 2 small bananas, chopped

Rocket Cake

The simple shapes and colour blocking of this cake make it look as if it was professionally made and who doesn't want that from a homemade cake? If you want, you can also cover the cake board in blue fondant icing and cut out white stars to complete the space scene. Our other space-themed birthday cake ideas include: a star, aliens, planets, an astronaut or even just an astronaut's helmet.

Lay the sponge on a large chopping board and cut out the rocket body shape (see photo opposite). Use the two large triangular pieces of sponge, trimmed off the top of the cake, as the rocket's wings.

Lay the cake in the rocket shape onto a serving plate or cake board and stick the side wings to the body of the rocket using some of the butter icing.

Cover the cake in a thin layer of butter icing to contain all the crumbs and create a smooth base for the fondant icing.

Dust the work surface with icing sugar and roll out the white fondant until it is approx. 1cm thick and large enough to cover the top of the cake, not including the side wings.

Place the icing across the top of the cake and with lightly sugared hands gently smooth the icing down the sides. Carefully trim any excess icing with a sharp knife.

Still on an icing sugar dusted surface, roll out the red fondant icing to approx. 1cm thick, then cut out a 4cm long triangle with curved edges for the nose of the rocket and two 8cm long deep triangles to cover the side wings.

Brush one side of the icing with apricot glaze and place it over the tip of the cake, smoothing down the sides as well. Repeat this process with the two larger triangles.

you will need

1 x 25 x 34cm rectangular White Chocolate Vanilla Sponge Cake (see recipe on page 16 but use half the quantity of ingredients)

500g White Butter Icing (see recipe page 17)

icing sugar, for dusting

500g white ready-made fondant icing

50g red ready-made fondant icing

2 tablespoons Apricot Glaze (see recipe page 17)

50g yellow ready-made fondant icing

50g blue ready-made fondant icing

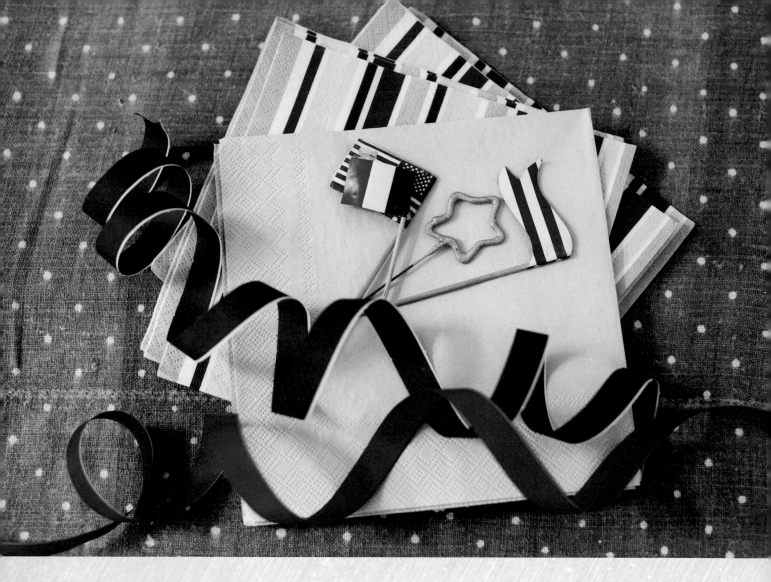

As before, roll out the yellow fondant icing to about 1cm thick and cut a 2cm wide strip. Brush one side of the strip with apricot glaze and place it horizontally, 10cm down from the top of the rocket.

As before, roll out the blue icing to about 1cm thick and cut two 1.5cm strips of icing. Brush one side of each of the strips with apricot glaze and place them either side of the yellow strip.

Stamp out three 2cm red circles from the remaining red icing with a cookie cutter. Brush one side of each of the circles with apricot glaze and place down the centre of the cake with a 1.5cm gap between each circle.

For an extra special start to the Happy Birthday singing and candle blowing, stick fountain candles into the bottom of the cake and light to represent the rocket flames. It's blast-off!

Alien Brew

SERVES 8

This drink was said to have been invented in 1874 and we haven't met a child that doesn't like it! It's called Alien Brew, so you get away with the frothy foamy treat being slightly odd looking.

Fill three-quarters of eight glasses with cola.

Carefully place a tablespoon of ice cream into each glass – be careful as it will froth up – and hand out to party guests.

you will need

2 litres cola
8 tablespoons vanilla ice cream

CIRCUS, CIRCUS

CIRCUS, CIRCUS

This is a wonderfully versatile theme for boys and girls of any age and is always a hit with adults too. Whether you are holding a party outside in the summer sun or indoors in mid-winter, it is a theme perfect for any season.

With animals, acrobatics and clowns to think about, there is no shortage of ideas when it comes to decorations, food and fancy dress. For the decorations, think bright colours, spots, stripes and use plenty of balloons and bunting to really set the scene. Hang streamers and party poppers from trees or mirrors, to add to the circus chaos and sprinkle generous amounts of confetti on the party table for yet more colour and flare. Depending on your budget, you can add an extra touch of magic by hiring a candyfloss or popcorn machine. These are available from online party hire companies and make a fabulous focal point. Try to rent one on wheels for easy manoeuvring and make sure there is an adult to take control of the machine and help serve the children.

As with all parties, set and agree a budget and make sure you've got enough time to prepare all the things, ahead of the day. If your budget allows, then booking a clown is often the first port of call for this theme but do check that your child actually wants one. It is amazing how many times we have witnessed terrified tears from the birthday boy or girl when faced with Coco the clown! Face-painters, magicians and jugglers are all popular choices, especially with children under four.

There is a huge array of cookie cutters available now – from big tops and elephants to acrobats and stars – so you should not have any problems finding appropriate shapes to make biscuits and sandwiches – just remember to make extra for any hungry parents or siblings.

Old-fashioned party games such as apple bobbing, sleeping lions, skittles and pin the tail on the elephant are all in keeping with the circus theme and will keep your guests entertained before and after they eat. For apple bobbing you will need to fill a large tub or bowl with water and add some apples. The players then have to 'catch' the apples with their teeth and without using their arms. To play sleeping lions, get all but one of the players to lie down on the floor with their eyes closed as if sleeping. The non-sleeping player walks around the others and tries to make them move without touching them. Any player caught moving stands up and joins the hunter. Piñatas are always a fabulous way to finish a party and come in all shapes and sizes. Just make sure you have a reasonable sized area and be prepared for a bit of mess!

Finally, instead of the traditional party bag, why not fill stripy paper sweetie bags with pick and mix sweets or old-fashioned toffees and bonbons to give to your guests as party favours. These not only look fabulous but they are certainly a cheap, yet fun option, which will please all your guests.

helter skelter sausages

This variation of a normal hot dog uses pastry instead of bread. These are easy to make and taste great dunked in tomato ketchup! For an added wow factor, display the sausages in colourful flowerpots or buckets.

Preheat the oven to 200°C/gas mark 6. Line a baking tray with baking parchment and set aside.

Working down the longest edge of the pastry, cut eight strips approx. 2.5cm wide.

Starting from the tip of the sausage, carefully wrap each pastry strip around and down a sausage in a helter-skelter style and lay on the lined baking tray. Bake in the oven for 25 minutes.

Meanwhile, trim a block of oasis so that it fits snuggly in a flowerpot or bucket. The oasis should sit 5cm below the top of the flowerpot rim. Cover the top of the oasis with a sheet of foil, tucking down the sides.

Remove the tray from the oven and lightly brush the pastry with the beaten egg, before returning for a further 10 minutes or until the pastry is golden.

Remove from the oven and leave to cool for 5 minutes. Using eight kebab sticks, carefully skewer the sausages and place upright in the flowerpot or bucket.

Serve immediately.

you will need

320g ready-rolled all-butter puff pastry sheet

8 good-quality pork chipolata sausages

1 large egg, beaten

Juggler's popcorn Bowls

No circus would be complete without a bag of popcorn! We have decided to stray from the traditional salt or sweet and have come up with a more original, cheesy flavour, which has been a hit at many of our parties.

Heat the oil in a large saucepan and sprinkle in the popping corn. Shake the pan to ensure all the kernels are coated in oil and cover with a tight-fitting lid. Reduce the heat and stand by for the popping!

As soon as the popping slows down, remove from the heat.

Pour the popcorn into a large bowl, (being careful not to include any unpopped kernels) and sprinkle the Parmesan and herbs over the top.

Stir well and leave to cool completely, before serving in brightly coloured bowls or divided up into cellophane bags tied with red and white ribbon.

you will need

4 tablespoons sunflower oil
150g popping corn
60g Parmesan, finely grated
1 teaspoon chopped fresh thyme

carnival stick cookies

★

These are one of our most popular treats. They are fun to make and look fabulous as table centrepieces. The decoration can be as simple or as elaborate as you want it to be. Or, if you prefer, you could make the cookies and let the children decorate their own during the party.

Preheat the oven to 190°C/gas mark 5. Line a baking tray with baking parchment and set aside.

In a large bowl, beat the butter and sugar together until pale and fluffy. Stir in the beaten egg, salt and vanilla extract.

Sift the flour and baking powder into the wet mixture in two batches and gently stir until the mixture forms a dough.

Roll the dough out onto a lightly floured surface until approx. 2.5cm thick. Using star cookie cutters, cut out shapes and place on the lined baking tray; you should get approx. 16 shapes out of this dough. Bake the cookies for 10 minutes until golden.

Remove from the oven and allow to cool for 5 minutes.

Carefully slide each cookie onto a wooden skewer to just over halfway up each cookie. Leave to cool completely, for about 2 hours, before decorating.

Roll the fondant icing out on a surface lightly dusted with icing sugar to a thickness of 1cm.

Using star cutters, stamp out icing shapes and lightly brush one side with a thin layer of apricot glaze. With the glaze-side down, gently place the icing on top of the cookie.

Using the writing icing tubes, cover one side of a Smartie and immediately stick onto the iced cookie. Repeat until all the cookies are covered in Smarties.

Once decorated, place the cookie sticks into a few empty jam jars or flowerpots to serve.

you will need

225g unsalted butter, softened
200g golden granulated sugar
1 large egg, beaten
pinch of salt
1 teaspoon vanilla extract
360g plain flour
1 teaspoon baking powder

to decorate

500g white ready-made fondant icing
Apricot Glaze (for recipe see page 17)
tubes of coloured writing icing
150g Smarties or other small coloured chocolates

toffee apple cupcakes

MAKES 48

Wow your little guests and tantalise their taste buds with these more-ish toffee apple cupcakes. The super-creamy mascarpone-based frosting sits atop a delicious apple sponge. We've found these are a real crowd pleaser.

Preheat the oven to 180°C/gas mark 4. Pop 48 mini paper cases into four mini cupcake tins, ready for filling.

Melt the butter in a small saucepan and leave to cool.

Put the grated apple into a bowl, add the sugar and melted butter and mix together. Add the eggs to the apple mixture and beat together until fully combined.

Sift together the dry ingredients and fold into the wet mixture.

Spoon the cake into the cases halfway up the sides and bake in the oven for 10–12 minutes or until golden.

Remove from the oven and leave the cupcakes in their tins for 15 minutes before transferring to a wire rack. Leave to cool completely before icing.

Put the mascarpone and icing sugar into a large bowl and beat together until well combined. Gently fold the dulce de leche into the mixture until it's a smooth and pipeable consistency.

Apply the topping to the cupcakes using a palette knife or a piping bag, whichever is easier for you.

Finally, sprinkle the toffee pieces over and transfer to a serving plate or cake stand.

for the cupcakes

150g salted butter

2 eating apples (e.g. Granny Smith), peeled and coarsely grated

150g soft brown sugar

2 medium eggs, beaten

200g self-raising flour

1 ½ teaspoons baking soda

1 teaspoon ground cinnamon

1 teaspoon ground ginger

½ teaspoon salt

for the frosting

250g mascarpone

200g icing sugar, sifted

1 heaped tablespoon dulce de leche

100g hard toffees, smashed

Elly Elephants

The assorted bright colours of these biscuits fit in perfectly with the Circus, Circus theme. Here, we have used a twist on a traditional shortbread recipe and married it with a modern but super-easy decorating technique. The shortbread can be made several days ahead of the party and stored in an airtight container, ready for decorating. The lavender smells wonderful, yet is subtle to taste. This is a good way of introducing children to new and diverse flavours.

Preheat the oven to 190°C/gas mark 5. Line two baking trays with baking parchment and set aside.

Beat together the sugar, butter, vanilla extract and honey until pale and fluffy. Stir in the flour and lavender until combined into a dough.

On a lightly floured surface, roll the dough to 1cm thick. Cut out 16 shortbread shapes with an elephant-shaped cutter. If you would like to use the biscuits as decorations, use the end of a straw to puncture a hole behind the elephant's head. Place on the lined baking trays.

Bake for 8–10 minutes until firm and golden. Remove from the oven and if needed, quickly re-puncture any holes that may have closed up during the cooking process. Leave to cool.

Melt the white chocolate in a heatproof bowl fitted over a pan of barely simmering water, making sure the bowl doesn't touch the water. Using a palette knife, spread a thin layer of the melted white chocolate over the top of the biscuits. Lay the chocolate-covered elephants onto greaseproof paper and carefully sprinkle each biscuit with hundreds and thousands or sugar strands. Leave for about 2 hours until the coating is set.

Store in an airtight container until ready to serve. Carefully thread ribbon through each hole and tie to make a loop, if desired.

you will need

55g golden caster sugar

125g salted butter, softened

1 teaspoon vanilla extract

1 tablespoon set (not clear) honey

180g plain flour, sifted

1 teaspoon dried lavender buds

For decoration

200g white chocolate, broken into pieces

80g hundreds and thousands

Ringmaster's nacho cups

MAKES 24 MINI NACHO CUPS ⭐

An all-time favourite that can be put together in minutes. You can be as experimental as you wish with nachos, so push the boundaries. Here we have given the old classic a Spanish kick by using slices of chorizo sausage and Manchego and cooked the filling in wonton wrappers instead of the traditional layered tortilla chips. Parents can feel pleased that the fresh tomato salsa is full of vitamins and antioxidants to keep their party guests happy and calm!

Preheat the oven to 200°C/gas mark 6.

Gently stir the salsa ingredients together in a bowl and set aside.

Lightly oil two 12-hole mini muffin trays and place a wonton wrapper in each hole, pressing them down against the sides, for a smooth finish.

Mix together the chorizo, cheese, crème fraîche, tomato purée and sweetcorn and fill each wonton cup with the mix so it is three-quarters full.

Bake the nachos in the oven for 20 minutes or until golden and bubbling.

Top with a teaspoon of salsa and serve warm.

for the salsa

150g cherry tomatoes, finely chopped
1 small onion, finely chopped
½ teaspoon caster sugar
juice of ½ lemon
4 basil leaves, finely chopped

for the nacho cups

sunflower oil, for greasing
24 wonton wrappers
120g chorizo sausage, cut into small chunks
200g Manchego, grated
3 tablespoons crème fraîche
1 tablespoon tomato purée
100g sweetcorn

clown cake

Take the fear out of clowns with this fun and friendly-looking clown cake. If you'd rather steer clear of a clown, other circus-themed birthday cake ideas to try include: a Big Top, elephant, juggling seal or spots, stars and stripes. You can buy great shaped cake tins and moulds to help with the more complicated designs (see Directory on page 204).

Sandwich the cakes together, using half the butter icing and carefully centre the cake on a 30.5cm round cake board.

Cover the cake completely, using the remaining butter icing, ensuring a smooth base for the fondant icing to rest on.

Lay the white fondant icing on a smooth work surface dusted with icing sugar. Roll the icing out until it is about 1cm thick and large enough to cover the top and sides of the cake.

Place the icing across the top of the cake and with lightly sugared hands, gently smooth it down the sides. Carefully trim any excess with a sharp knife.

Now that you have the clown's head, you can have fun decorating the face and sorting the hair. Fondant icing can be dyed any colour you wish and you can create some great marbled effects by mixing and rolling a little of each different coloured icing together. Icing pens are easy to find (see page 204) and you can use these to add as much or as little detail as you want. They are especially useful for drawing outlines for lips or eyes/eyelashes.

you will need

2 x 20cm round White Chocolate Vanilla Sponge Cakes (see recipe on page 16)

500g White Butter Icing (see page 17)

500g white ready-made fondant icing

icing sugar, for dusting

1 small black icing pen

extra sweets and items for decoration (see overleaf)

Below are a few of our ideas for inspiration:

Hair – candy floss, strawberry bootlaces, Cheerios cereal, decorating sugar (any colour), popcorn, candy necklaces, pomegranate seeds.

Hat – cut a trianguar piece of fondant icing, leave to dry overnight then stick onto the cake using icing pens.

Eyes – pretzels, halved Oreo cookies, Smarties or other small coloured chocolates, marshmallows, iced ring biscuits, giant chocolate buttons.

Nose – a teacake (either left brown or covered with some red icing), glacé cherry, large fresh strawberry, a mini iced cupcake.

Mouth – liquorice strips, red Smarties, raspberries.

MUNGO'S MONKEY SHAKE

SERVES 8

This easy and quick banana smoothie recipe can be made a few hours ahead of time and left to chill in a large jug in the fridge, until needed. A teaspoon of good-quality chocolate powder can be added for a chocolatey twist and a few fresh raspberries on the top of the glass is always a welcome and pretty surprise.

Place the banana, milk, sugar, vanilla extract and cinnamon in a blender. Whizz until smooth.

Divide between eight small glasses and decorate with a few raspberries.

you will need

4 large bananas, peeled and sliced

1 litre semi-skimmed milk

30g soft brown sugar

1 tablespoon vanilla extract

1 teaspoon cinnamon

a couple of handfuls of fresh raspberries, to decorate

WILD, WILD WEST

WILD, WILD WEST

In the early days of Hats & Bells, we both considered the Wild, Wild West theme more appropriate for boys but we have been proved wrong on many occasions. If you have a substantial number of girls attending a longed-for cowboy party, then do not worry. Girls are just as keen to get dressed up in their cowgirl boots and checked shirts. Some go a step further and head down the can-can dancer route, complete with feather boas and petticoats. To get your guests in the mood, on arrival, present each one with a sheriff's badge (these can be bought online very cheaply) and give them each a name for the afternoon, for example: Maverick, Miss Dolly, Bullseye, Cowboy Buck etc.

Setting the scene for such a party is, thankfully, straightforward and if you have the time and inclination, then many things can be handmade in minimal time and at little cost. Use thick pieces of cardboard to make appropriate road signs and directions, which you can then hang around the party room or garden. For example 'BLACKSMITHS', 'HOT BATHS 5 CENTS', 'JAIL', 'SALOON OPEN'. Play about with fonts on your computer for inspiration and use different coloured paints for each sign. If you are a computer whizz, then try your hand at designing a 'WANTED' poster with a picture of the birthday boy or girl on it. If this is beyond your computer capability, then you can easily find free downloads for 'WANTED' posters or buy them from online party stores and simply stick photographs onto the posters

yourself. It's great to print these posters as large as possible (A3, for example) and cut out the square where the photo normally goes. Then you can capture each of the party guests in turn, holding the poster with their faces being the villain at large. They would make great thank you cards.

Cactuses, mini hay bales and bundles of hanging horseshoes really help set the scene and if you would like a fiesta kick to your party, then do invest in some mini maracas, large sombreros and colourful horse-shaped piñatas. Decorate the table with cowboy confetti (available at party shops), rubber snakes, multicoloured feathers and piles of chocolate gold coins.

There are so many games options. Consider staging a tug of war between cowboys and Indians (this is definitely better suited to the outdoors). An archery competition is always popular but just make sure you have an adult monitoring the game at all times. Although your little ones are probably not yet familiar with the rules of poker, setting up a card table and having Snap or Beggar Thy Neighbour card games, always goes down well, especially with any younger children. You could hire a magician to teach the children simple card tricks too – just make sure there are no more than four children in each group.

A game we have fond to be popular is 'Tenderfoot', which is best done outdoors. Gather your guests into a circle and allow the

birthday boy or girl to stand in the middle, holding a broomstick. He/she will be known as 'The Sheriff'. The Sheriff must then swing the stick around the circle of children, sometimes aiming low and sometimes high. All the guests must avoid being touched by the broom and jump or duck under it. The Sheriff can change the direction of the broom at any point, so you have to stay alert! The last one standing is the winner and then becomes the new 'High Sheriff'.

Keep food presentation simple and rustic. Rough and ready is our motto for this theme, so invest in some large wooden chopping boards and slates and just pile the food high. If using slates, write the name of each food in one corner using a piece of chalk and finish with

mini American toothpick flags or other appropriate cupcake toppers (these are available from well-stocked party shops).

For the party bags, fill little canvas bags with gold chocolate coins, bandanas, felt moustaches and toy water pistols. Or, if you cleared out your local garden centre of their mini-cactus supply, then do hand these out as going home presents. In advance of the party, ask your birthday boy/girl to write and decorate little labels with each guest's name on. Then simply loop these prepared labels over each cactus before the children leave the party. These make a wonderful change from the norm and parents will thank you for a more peaceful, sugar-free journey home!

tear and share bread

SERVES 10–12

Annabel stumbled across this delicious yet simple idea while in
Maryland and it has gone down a storm at every party. We
have made it child-friendly by using pancetta rather than spicy
salami but any deli meat or cooked and shredded meat will
work well, so have fun experimenting.

Preheat the oven to 180°C/gas mark 4. Lightly oil a baking tray
and set aside.

Without cutting through the bottom crust, cut the bread
lengthways and then widthways (creating a grid pattern). It can
be quite tricky but don't worry, the bread is very forgiving.

Using your fingers, massage the cream cheese into all the
cracks, followed by the pancetta cubes. Scatter the Cheddar
into all the slits and finish with the chopped basil.

Put the loaf onto the baking tray and bake for 20 minutes or
until the cheese is melted and bubbling.

Allow to cool for 5 minutes before serving on a wooden
chopping board. Let your guests tear off a chunk – it tastes
great dipped into the Ranch Dressing on page 157 too.

you will need

sunflower oil, for greasing

1 round loaf of sourdough bread

150g cream cheese

150g pancetta cubes, lightly
 cooked

250g medium Cheddar, grated

5 basil leaves, roughly chopped

crispy potato skins

★

Years ago there was a very unglamorous, yet seriously delicious roadside restaurant called The Klondike. During the long school holidays, all the local mums (including Annabel's) would swarm there with their children, where they'd feast on 'Dawson City Chicken Fingers' and the best 'Crispy Tatty Skins' known to man! Although The Klondike has sadly long since gone, here is an attempt at replicating their delicious signature dish… viva la Klondike!

Preheat the oven to 200°C/gas mark 6.

Wash the potatoes, dry with kitchen paper and brush with a little olive oil. Place the potatoes on a baking tray and bake for an hour or until they are golden brown and soft.

Remove the potatoes from the oven and cut each one lengthways. Then, using a spoon, scoop out the insides of the potato, leaving approx. 1cm of potato flesh on the skin. Lay the potato skins on a baking tray.

Mix the scooped-out potato with the butter and mozzarella and replace equally back into each of the potato skins.

Scatter with a generous handful of the cooked bacon, before placing back into the oven for 10 minutes or until the cheese is bubbling and the bacon crispy.

Remove from the oven and, using tongs, place the skins on a serving plate or big wooden chopping board and serve.

you will need

8 medium baking potatoes
olive oil, for brushing
30g butter
180g mozzarella, grated
200g bacon cubes, cooked

Sizzling Fajitas with Easy Peasy Salsa

SERVES 8

This quick and easy recipe will have every Speedy Gonzalez in whoops of joy. If your guests would like a bit more of a kick in their fajitas, just add half a teaspoon of paprika to the spice list. 'Arriba, arriba, andale, andale!'

Heat a little olive oil in a large non-stick frying pan, add the chicken and cook for 6–7 minutes or until tender. (Depending on how large the pan is, you might have to do this is two batches.) Add the peppers and onions and cook for a further 5–10 minutes until the vegetables are soft and the chicken golden in colour.

Tip the lemon juice, oregano and spices into the pan and mix together well before removing from the heat. Cover with foil and leave to stand for 5 minutes.

Meanwhile, make the salsa. Place all the ingredients into a small bowl and gently whisk together, seasoning to taste. To make it a bit sweeter, you can always add a good squirt of tomato ketchup or a little more sugar.

Lay the tortillas on a flat surface or on individual plates. Add one tablespoon of salsa to the centre of each tortilla and using the back of a spoon, spread the salsa over the entire tortilla. Next, take a generous spoonful of chicken mix and place it on the left-hand side of the tortilla. Top with a teaspoon of sour cream and a little grated cheese. Gently fold the bottom (edge nearest you) up by 7.5cm, before tightly rolling up the sides, going from left to right. Cut in half and serve immediately.

you will need

olive oil, for cooking

6 boneless chicken breasts, cut into 5cm strips

1 red pepper, thinly sliced

1 yellow pepper, thinly sliced

2 medium onions, thinly sliced

juice of 1 lemon

2 tablespoons dried oregano

½ teaspoon ground cumin

½ teaspoon ground cinnamon

8 tortillas, warmed

100g Cheddar or Monterey Jack, grated

250ml sour cream

For the easy peasy salsa

400g can chopped tomatoes, well drained

½ red onion, finely chopped

a handful of fresh parsley, chopped

2 tablespoons lime juice

1 garlic clove, finely chopped

pinch of soft brown sugar

salt and freshly ground black pepper

Finger Lickin' Ribs

MAKES 16

See if your little cowboys or cowgirls can eat these juicy ribs without licking their lips, cheeks or fingers...we can't and we've been trying for years! Just make sure you have a good supply of napkins at the ready for clear-up time.

Place the ribs in a large bowl.

Mix the olive oil, vinegar, tomato ketchup and brown sugar together and pour over the ribs. Cover with clingfilm and leave to marinate for 3 hours in the fridge.

Preheat the oven to 200°C/gas mark 6.

Once marinated, remove the clingfilm and roast the ribs for 1 hour, basting with the marinade every 20 minutes.

While the ribs are cooking, make the ranch dressing by combining the yogurt, crème fraîche, lemon juice and parsley in a wide bowl.

Once the ribs are cooked through, remove from the oven and serve them piled high on a wooden board or large rectangular slate, with the sauce on the side.

you will need

2 tablespoons olive oil

1 teaspoon malt vinegar

6 tablespoons tomato ketchup

1 heaped tablespoon dark brown sugar

16 pork spare ribs

for the ranch dressing

3 tablespoons Greek yogurt

3 tablespoons crème fraîche

1 teaspoon lemon juice

1 small bunch fresh parsley, chopped

Drop scone Horseshoes

MAKES 12–15 ⋯⋯⋯⋯⋯⋯⋯⋯⋯⋯⋯⋯ ★

This recipe was handed down to Hatty by her grandmother, as these were always a firm favourite at family get-togethers. Drop scones are basically pancakes and children of all ages can get involved in some part of the cooking process. We have used maple syrup and blueberries in this recipe but these are also delicious served with fruit compôte, warmed jam or just butter and honey.

Place the butter, golden syrup and 2 tablespoons of water into a non-stick saucepan and melt over a low heat. Once smooth, remove from the heat and set aside.

In a large mixing bowl, beat the egg and milk together before stirring in the melted butter mixture.

Add the flour to the mixture and beat together until it is a decent thickness – you want the batter to be able to hold together and not run away in the frying pan; a double-cream-like thickness is the aim.

Heat a teaspoon of oil in a non-stick frying pan and using a tablespoon, pour a generous amount of mixture into the pan, in a horseshoe shape. (To do this, start from the top left side of the horseshoe, sweep down and up, to complete the shape.)

Cook until small bubbles begin to appear and the underside is golden, before flipping over and cooking on the other side for a further 30 seconds. Place on a warm plate, in a warm oven and then repeat this process until you have used all the mixture.

The pancakes will not be uniform in shape but if you like things neat, then you can always trim the edges with scissors before serving.

Pile the horseshoes up onto a serving plate, before drizzling with the maple syrup and scattering with the fresh blueberries. Serve immediately.

you will need

30g salted butter
1 tablespoon golden syrup
1 egg, beaten
100ml semi-skimmed milk
4 tablespoons self-raising flour, sifted
vegetable oil, for frying

to serve

4 tablespoons maple syrup
100g fresh blueberries

apple nachos

★

Well, this is certainly one way of enticing your children to the fruit bowl! Made to look like a plate of nachos, this recipe is always admired by our clients for its originality and simplicity. However, if the thought of the effects of all those chocolate drops and marshmallows fills you with horror, simply scatter the apples with fresh berries, dried fruit or yogurt-covered raisins, for a slightly healthier alternative.

Pour the lemon juice into a small bowl.

Cut the apples into 2.5cm horizontal slices. Immediately dip each slice into the lemon juice and set aside.

Pour the butterscotch sauce into a small saucepan and place over a low heat until it begins to simmer, about 3–4 minutes.

Arrange the apple slices in layers on a large, round serving plate.

Drizzle the butterscotch sauce over the apples before scattering with the marshmallows and chocolate chips. Serve immediately and shout Yeehah! while you're at it!

you will need

juice of 2 large lemons

8 Granny Smith apples, cored

100g butterscotch or toffee sauce

100g mini marshmallows

50g white chocolate chips

50g dark or milk chocolate chips

mama's cherry pies

SERVES 8 ★

Is there anything more comforting than the smell of a home-baked pie? Perhaps there'd be less shoot-outs if people baked and ate more pie?! We can only wonder but these pies warm the hearts of all who taste them. We've used fresh cherries in this recipe but apple, cinnamon and blackberries make a delicious alternative for those colder months. Why not bake star-shaped pies for any high sheriffs you might be expecting for tea?

Preheat the oven to 180°C/gas mark 4. Line a baking tray with baking parchment.

In a bowl, gently mix together the mascarpone, cherry pieces and jam. Set aside.

On a lightly floured surface, unroll the pastry and stamp out 16 heart shapes, using a 6cm heart-shaped cookie cutter.

Place a heaped teaspoon of the cherry mixture in the centre of each of eight hearts.

Lightly brush the remaining eight pastry hearts with beaten egg and lay them on top of the cherry mix.

Brush the surface of each pie with the egg and using a fork gently crimp the edges, sealing the two pastry sheets together. Prick each pie in the centre with a fork.

Place on the baking tray and bake for 15 minutes or until golden.

Remove from the oven and leave to cool for 10 minutes, before dusting with icing sugar and serving.

you will need

100g mascarpone

140g fresh cherries, pitted and finely chopped and drained

1 tablespoon raspberry jam

320g ready-rolled shortcrust pastry sheet

1 large egg, beaten

icing sugar, for dusting

sheriff's Badge cake

A sheriff's badge is a great cake to choose if you are after something easy to personalise for the birthday boy or girl. Using icing pens you can simply write their name, age, local town, city or school and decorate with anything from gold and silver dragées to Smarties, glitter and chocolate buttons. Our other Wild, Wild West birthday cake ideas include: a cowboy boot, cactus or a cake decorated with a paisley bandana or blue denim and cow print.

Draw a star with round points, as on a sheriff's badge on paper – this will be your template for the cake. The star should be about 22cm and the round ends 2cm circles.

Lay the cooled sponges on a large chopping board and, using the template and a sharp knife, cut out the sheriff badge shape from both sponge cakes.

Sandwich the cakes together, using 3 tablespoons of the butter icing and carefully centre the cake on a 30.5cm round cake board.

Place the remaining butter icing in a mixing bowl and add a couple of drops of yellow food colouring. Mix thoroughly until there are no streaks. Cover the sheriff badge in a layer of the yellow butter icing. Dip a palette knife into boiling water and smooth over the cake.

Lay the blue fondant icing on a smooth work surface dusted with icing sugar. Roll the icing out until it is about 1.5cm thick and cut out a 10cm disc (a side plate makes a great template) and six 2cm discs with a pastry cutter.

Place the large disc in the middle of the Sheriff's Badge cake and the smaller circles on the rounded points of the star.

you will need

1 x 25 x 34cm rectangular White Chocolate Vanilla Sponge Cake (see recipe on page 16 but use half the quantity of ingredients)

1 x 25 x 34cm rectangular Chocolate Sponge Cake (see recipe on page 16 but use half the quantity of ingredients)

500g White Butter Icing (see recipe page 17)

50g blue ready-made fondant icing

icing sugar, for dusting

50g yellow ready-made fondant icing

500g Smarties or other small coloured chocolates

Stick Smarties or other small coloured chocolates around the outside edge of the star and around the outside edge of the blue fondant disc, covering the join line.

Roll the yellow fondant icing out until it is about 1cm thick. Using letter and number cookie cutters, stamp out the birthday boy or girl's name and their age.

Arrange the letters and numbers on the blue central disc. Use water to stick the fondant letters and numbers to the icing. It looks great if you curve the letters around the circle – Sheriff around the top, the age in the middle and the child's name around the bottom.

the gunslinger

SERVES 8

These drinks can be put together half an hour or so before your party starts and just kept in the fridge with the lids tightly sealed to stay cool and fizzy. Use blue gingham for the boys and pink for the girls or simply label the jars with each of your guests' names.

Combine the orange juice and the ginger ale in a 2.5 litre jug.

Put a couple of ice cubes into eight 250g jam jars and pour the gunslinger into each one. Add a slice of orange and replace the lid of the jar.

Top each jam jar with a piece of gingham cloth and fix with either an elastic band or a piece of raffia or ribbon.

you will need

1 litre orange juice, freshly squeezed, no bits

1 litre ginger ale

16 ice cubes, to serve

1 orange, thinly sliced into 8

GHOSTS, GHOULS AND GOBLINS

GHOSTS, GHOULS AND GOBLINS

If you want to bring out your inner creative demon, then this chapter offers piles of inspiration for a spooktacular party or classic Halloween celebration. (Most of the recipes are easy and fun to make with your children.) From veiny eggs to make your guests wince to impressive edible graveyards. You'll have all you need and much, much more.

Fancy dress is a must for this kind of party and if you baulk at the idea of sewing your own costume, then you need look no further than large supermarkets for inspiration. Halloween outfits appear as early as August, so you can get the pick of the pile if you plan ahead.

Face-painters can add an extra-realistic dimension to such parties. Who's up for a green witch's face complete with giant warts? Don't worry if your budget doesn't stretch to professional face-painters, you can do a great job yourself or – for even scarier results – allow each child to decorate their own face. If you're going for this option, isolate an area where you can protect the carpet and surrounding furniture. Place various colours of face paint on the table with a few sponges and a couple of brushes, complete with some free-standing mirrors and watch as the little terrors transform themselves before your very eyes. Just be on stand by with a generous supply of baby wipes, to mop up the excesses.

Get your guests in the mood from the off, by greeting all visitors with a doorstep decorated with carved pumpkins and candles

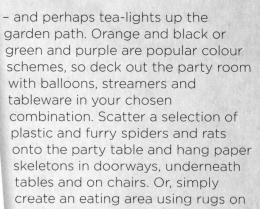

– and perhaps tea-lights up the garden path. Orange and black or green and purple are popular colour schemes, so deck out the party room with balloons, streamers and tableware in your chosen combination. Scatter a selection of plastic and furry spiders and rats onto the party table and hang paper skeletons in doorways, underneath tables and on chairs. Or, simply create an eating area using rugs on

the floor and dot cardboard cut-out haunted houses, around the periphery.

Themed window stickers and cobwebs help set the scene and can be bought cheaply online, along with life-size cut-outs and hanging spider and bat decorations. In our experience, these parties tend to be action packed and sweetie-fuelled, so consider having a buffet instead of a sit-down party tea.

There are endless games to suit this theme, and here are few of our client's favourites:

For 'Make a Mummy', split your guests into teams of three or four. They then have 2 minutes to mummify a team member from head to toe, using just toilet roll. The neatest and most convincing mummy wins.

'Ghost Face' is messy but oh-so-much fun! Fill a plastic bowl with icing sugar (you will probably need three or four packs but be sure to hold some back so you can top up the bowl as the game continues). Bury marshmallows or jelly snakes in the sugar mound and give each child 30 seconds to pull out as many treats at they

can with their mouths only – no hands! Whoever demolishes the most sweets is the winner. This game is best saved for the end of a party to avoid spoiling painted faces and costumes!

Finally, for home-based parties 'Ghost Hunter' is a must. Hide an inflatable ghost somewhere in your house and turn out all the lights. Split your guests into teams of three and supply each leader with a torch. The first team to find the inflatable, wins.

Be sure to stash prizes into suitably decorated vessesl; a cauldron, witch's hat or upturned skull would all be great.

Toy shops are packed with suitable 'going home' presents to fit this theme. Rather than stuffing bags full of sweets, hand-pick those items that fit the bill for maximum impact – anything from squishy eyeball stress balls and trinkets of fake blood to Dracula fangs and zombie masks. With so much fun to be had, you really can let your imagination run riot – and do share the fun and involve the birthday boy or girl in the preparations, too.

veiny Devilled eggs

We had the idea to create a Halloween treat from marbled eggs when we came across the marvellous Asian tea eggs, which are dyed in a spiced tea liquid. The colour in our marbled eggs doesn't add flavour but the results are wondrous and fit a spooky party no end. You can use any colour combinations you want or simply match your colour scheme.

Once the boiled eggs have been drained and cooled, tap each egg carefully with the back of a spoon to crack the shells; you want the shell to remain attached, so don't crack them too hard.

Fill eight heatproof tumblers (big enough to fit an egg inside) two thirds full with boiling water. Pour a teaspoon of green food colouring into four tumblers and stir. Repeat this process with the purple food colouring and the remaining four tumblers of water. Carefully place one egg into each tumbler and leave to stand for 20 minutes.

Remove the eggs from the tumblers and rinse under cold running water before patting dry with some kitchen paper.

Carefully peel the eggs, leaving the membrane intact. Cut the top 4cm off the egg, remove the yolks and set aside in a bowl. Then take a small slice from the bottom of the egg, so that it can sit on a plate. Repeat this process with the remaining eggs.

Add the mayonnaise to the egg yolks and mash together with a fork. Using a small spoon, carefully scoop the mixture back into the egg whites.

Place the eggs on a black plate to serve.

You will need

8 large eggs, hard-boiled

280ml boiling water

4 teaspoons green food colouring

4 teaspoons purple food colouring

3 tablespoons mayonnaise

Autumnal Leaves

SERVES 8

These vegetable crisps are crunchy and delicious. They are a great alternative to packets of potato crisps and the colourful assortment of vegetables is perfect for the autumn theme. These look fantastic served in hollowed-out small pumpkins, marrows or little baskets.

Preheat the oven 190°C/gas mark 5.

With a potato peeler or mandolin, carefully and thinly slice the potatoes and parsnips lengthways, before drying well with kitchen paper and placing into a large mixing bowl.

Using a sharp knife, cut the beetroot into thin slices (the thinner the better). Dry with kitchen paper and place in a separate mixing bowl.

Add three quarters of the oil, 1 teaspoon of the herbs and a good pinch of salt to the potatoes and parsnips and, using your hands, gently mix together, until all the slices are well coated. Repeat this process with the beetroot slices, using the remaining oil, herbs and again a good pinch of salt.

Place the vegetables in a single layer onto baking trays keeping the beetroot on a separate baking tray as they will take longer to cook.

Bake the sweet potato and parsnips for about 20 minutes or until golden and crispy. Watch them carefully so they don't burn.

Leave the beetroot crisps in the oven for a further 15–20 minutes but again keep an eye on them.

Once all the vegetables are out of the oven, place them onto a wire rack to cool. The vegetable crisps can be kept in an airtight container for up to three days.

Place in a small hollowed-out pumpkin or baskets to serve.

you will need

2 sweet potatoes, peeled

2 parsnips, peeled

2 beetroot, peeled

6 tablespoons sunflower oil

salt

2 teaspoons dried mixed herbs

small pumpkin, hollowed, to serve (optional)

Dracula's stew

SERVES 8-10

We first made this for a client's Halloween party in 2010 and ever since it has been one of our bestsellers. As well as being a perfect winter warmer, it can be made ahead of time and simply reheated on the hob.

Chop the sausages into 5cm pieces.

Heat the oil in a frying pan and add the sausages and chopped onions. Lightly fry together until the sausages are golden brown on all sides. Remove the pan from the heat and set aside.

In a medium saucepan, add the canned tomatoes, stock, chutney, tomato purée and fresh basil. Gently bring to the boil before reducing the heat and leaving the sauce to simmer for 20 minutes, or until it has reduced by about a third and thickened. Stir occasionally.

Add the sausages and onions to the sauce and simmer for a further 15 minutes.

Stir in the chickpeas and taste, adding any additional seasoning as necessary.

Remove from the heat and serve in individual mugs with crusty buttered bread or ciabatta or serve on plates with a buttery root vegetable mash. However you choose to serve it, it'll be devoured in no time.

you will need

16 good-quality pork sausages

1 tablespoon olive oil

2 large red onions, finely chopped

2 x 400g cans chopped tomatoes

450ml chicken or vegetable stock

2 tablespoons mango chutney

2 tablespoons tomato purée

a handful of fresh basil, torn

400g can chickpeas, drained

salt and freshly ground back pepper

crusty bread, ciabatta or root vegetable mash, to serve

vampire pots

SERVES 8

As these showstoppers can be made a day ahead of the party, enlist the help of the birthday boy or girl to make these little pots of chocolateyness. For the full graveyard effect, arrange in a line along the party table.

Melt the chocolate in a heatproof bowl over a pan of barely simmering water, making sure the bowl doesn't touch the water.

Add the egg yolks to the melted chocolate and stir to combine.

In a separate bowl, and using an electric whisk, whisk the egg whites until they form soft peaks.

Fold the egg whites into the melted chocolate, one spoonful at a time, being careful not to beat the mixture. Once combined, spoon into eight pots (150ml are a perfect size) and put in the fridge for 3 hours to set.

Cut the sponge fingers in half widthways and using an icing pen, write a ghostly message on each biscuit (for example: RIP); these become the graves' headstones.

Remove the pots from the fridge and place a jelly snake in each one, ensuring the head is sticking out of the top of the mousse.

Take a sponge finger and place upright in the mousse. Repeat this process for each pot.

Generously sprinkle the Oreo cookie crumbs on top of the pots and return to the fridge for a further 30 minutes or until ready to serve.

you will need

250g good-quality dark chocolate (minimum 70 per cent cocoa solids), broken into pieces

3 large eggs, separated

4 sponge fingers

1 black icing pen

8 jelly snake sweets

8 Oreo cookies, crumbled (centre filling removed)

chocolate pumpkins

MAKES 12

These are, quite simply, heavenly – or should that be devilishly good? By cooking the chocolate mixture inside a fresh orange, the fondant is infused with the fruity flavour, resulting in a gooey chocolate orange treat. Not only do they look like mini pumpkins, they taste delicious too. Feel free to use black icing pens to decorate typical pumpkin faces onto the oranges – in fact, the kids could do their own. Make sure you have made a few extra for any hungry parents.

Preheat the oven to 200°C/gas mark 6.

Cut the top (approx. 2cm) off the oranges (reserving these for later) and hollow out the middle, leaving a small amount of flesh at the bottom. Set aside.

Put the caster sugar and butter in a mixing bowl and cream together until light and fluffy.

Add the eggs and beat, before adding the flour and cocoa powder. Mix together until combined.

Place 1 level tablespoon of mixture into each orange and place on a baking tray. If the orange doesn't stand upright, use crumpled foil to prop it up. Bake for 15 minutes.

Remove from the oven and replace the orange lids on top of the chocolate fondant and serve immediately.

you will need

12 oranges
150g golden caster sugar
150g salted butter, softened
3 medium eggs
110g self-raising flour
40g cocoa powder

Naan Ghost Pizzas

MAKES 12 ★

Using naan breads as bases, these cheesy ghosts make a welcome difference from your standard Italian pizza. We have simply used three toppings in this recipe but as for any pizza, anything goes! If your little ones have exotic taste buds, experiment with different cheeses – blue, goats', sheeps' – and you can always dot on some spinach, mushrooms or cherry tomatoes in the toppings, for a slightly healthier spin.

Preheat the oven to 200°C/gas mark 6. Lightly grease two baking trays.

Using a 7.5cm ghost cookie cutter, stamp out three ghosts from each naan bread and lay onto the baking trays.

In a bowl, mix together the tomato purée and pesto until well combined.

Using a palette knife, spread a tablespoon of the mixture onto each ghost shape, ensuring you reach and cover the edges.

Next, take a small handful of mozzarella for each ghost and sprinkle evenly over the surface, followed by a few pieces of chorizo or ham.

Finally, take two olive halves and position them as the ghost's eyes.

Repeat this process for all the ghosts before placing in the oven for 10 minutes, or until the cheese is golden and bubbling. Serve immediately.

you will need

oil, for greasing

4 naan breads

6 tablespoons tomato purée

6 tablespoons good-quality red pesto

150g mozzarella, grated

150g chorizo or honey-roasted ham, cut into small chunks

12 pitted black olives, halved

spooktacular ghost cake

SERVES 10–12

Many of the cakes for this theme work better if you have a mould (see Directory on page 204). However, you can still make a fun and spooky creation with a normal round or rectangular tin and add the decorations on top – as we do here with our ghost cake. Other popular cake ideas we have for this theme include: a haunted house, pumpkin, spider or mummy.

Using a ruler, measure an equal height halfway up the cake and insert at least four toothpicks horizontally and evenly spaced, just below the measured spot. Cut the cake with a serrated knife just above the toothpicks.

Carefully lift the top half off the cake and place the bottom half of the sponge centrally on a 30.5cm round cake board, securing in place with a dab of chocolate butter icing.

Take 3 heaped tablespoons of chocolate butter icing and spread it evenly over the sponge cake on the board, before carefully sandwiching the cakes back together.

Cover the cake in a thin layer of chocolate butter icing to contain the crumbs and create a smooth base for the fondant icing. Leave to set for an hour at room temperature.

Dust the work surface with icing sugar and roll out the purple fondant until it is approx. 1cm thick and large enough to cover the top and sides of the cake.

Place the icing across the top of the cake and with lightly sugared hands, gently smooth the icing down the sides. Carefully trim any excess icing with a sharp knife.

Cut each mini roll in half and set aside.

Now, roll out the white fondant icing, on a lightly dusted work surface, until it is approx. 1cm thick and cut out three 8cm circles with a pastry cutter.

you will need

1 x 20cm round Chocolate Sponge Cake (see recipe page 16)

500g Chocolate Butter Icing (see recipe page 17)

icing sugar, for dusting

500g purple ready-made fondant icing

2 chocolate mini rolls

30g white ready-made fondant icing

1 black icing pen

silver glitter, to sprinkle

Place the circle of icing over three of the half mini rolls. Don't worry about folds and pleats, these are your mini ghosts! The remaining half mini roll will not be used, so that's your reward as cake-maker or perhaps offer to a little helper.

With an icing pen, draw black oval eyes and a circular mouth onto each ghost. Then, using a small dot of chocolate butter icing as the glue, carefully stick each ghost on top of the cake.

Next, sprinkle over some edible glitter; don't use sparingly, this is a cake that should sparkle from a distance.

If you want to add more than just the ghosts, why not cut out some stars or ghost shapes with cookie cutters using any remaining fondant icing. An orange or purple ribbon around the cake always add a great finishing touch.

slimy lime grime

This tastes mainly of lemonade but the jelly creates a nasty globby and slimy texture, which your little terrors will love! Simply swap to a red jelly if you would rather create a bloody thirst quencher.

Chop the jelly into little chunks and put into a measuring jug. Add the boiling water.

Stir the jelly for about 30 seconds (you don't want it to completely dissolve).

Pour the lemonade into a clear plastic jug and add the green jelly mixture and stir gently.

When you pour the liquid into glasses, use a ladle to scoop out some of the jelly globs and add a few to each glass.

you will need

2 x 135g packets lime jelly
150ml boiling water
2 litres lemonade

LAST-MINUTE PANIC PARTY

LAST-MINUTE PANIC PARTY

If you're reading this chapter, then we already know that time is of the essence. Parents finding themselves running out of time ahead of a party is not unusual. We've often been asked to organise parties less than 48 hours beforehand and although it can be stressful, it is possible and often these mad-dash events are the most fun.

The menu ideas suggested here are simple, foolproof and we have chosen them in the hope that most of our readers can easily find the majority of the ingredients in their store cupboard or at least in their local supermarket.

Children will love making their own pizzas and ice cream sundaes and this will take up some of the party entertainment time, so a bonus for parents pushed to have organised other games too! (To avoid chaos, divide your guests into groups of four to six for their time in the kitchen and keep the children well away from the oven.) Make sure that all the topping ingredients for both the pizza and ice cream bar are laid out in little bowls before the party starts and are clearly labelled. (Do check that there are no allergies among the party group.) If your little one is a chef in the making, then why not make it a cooking party? You can always buy ready-made cookie dough and kill an hour or two, with giant cookie or cupcake baking and decorating as well.

The no-cook birthday cake is incredibly versatile and can be made three hours or three days before the party. It takes all of 15 minutes to put together and can be decorated with any sweets, so choose the birthday boy or girl's favourites – just be sure to have some candles.

Thankfully, most good-sized supermarkets are now well stocked with tableware, decorations, balloons and party bag fillers, so do not worry if there is no time to order anything online. (Although most online stores can guarantee a next-day delivery service but be prepared to pay double for postage.) Lollipops and bumper bags of mini chocolate bars are perfect to pad out any party bags and to give away as prizes. For easy table decorations, scatter sweets all over the party table and attach a balloon with a name tag on to the back of each child's chair.

Three popular games which can be organised last minute and require no tools or utensils are: Charades, Wink Murder and Sardines. A dance competition is always hilarious fun too and a great way of building up your guests' appetites. If you have 20 minutes to spare before the party, quickly prep for a game of Who am I? For this, you'll need some sticky labels and a pen. Write down a famous person's name on each label (be quite certain that your little guests will be familiar with these people – cartoon characters are always a safe bet, politicians are not!) and as each guest arrives, stick a label onto their forehead, ensuring they don't see the name. Then, once everyone has arrived, sit in a circle and let your guests take it in turns to ask six questions about who they are, before they must guess. The person who asks the least number of questions and guesses their character correctly, wins. A great way to end the party, is with a few cans of silly string. This stuff is a real hit with children but perhaps, if the weather allows it, take the foamy action outside to save your home from ruin!

DIY Pizzas

Most kids love to cook, so no doubt you'll have a queue of willing pizza-makers. Whether they want a simple Margherita or something more adventurous, they can choose from the tempting toppings on offer and create their own masterpiece.

Preheat the oven to 180°C/gas mark 4.

Give each child a pizza base and a ramekin with a little of the tomato sauce in it. Ask the children to carefully spread the sauce onto their bases, leaving a 1cm border around the edge.

Place all the other topping ingredients in bowls and let the children add whatever they wish to their individual pizza.

Place the assembled pizzas onto a non-stick baking tray. Bake for 15 minutes or until the cheese is golden and bubbling, and the base is cooked through. Cook the pizzas in batches and don't worry if some cool down, children don't like piping hot pizzas.

Cut into quarters and serve immediately.

you will need

8 ready-made pizza bases (between 20–25cm)

350g jar of pizza tomato sauce

200g mild Cheddar, grated

200g mozzarella, grated

1 red pepper, thinly sliced

1 yellow pepper, thinly sliced

120g honey-roasted ham, chopped or pepperoni slices

150g button mushrooms, sliced

45g olives, pitted

veggie Dip pots

These are deliciously fresh and healthy and little guests love to pick and choose their food and relish the dipping too. If you haven't got time to make the sauce, then pick up a dip selection at your local supermarket. Anything goes, so choose whatever will keep your little guests happy.

First, gently mix together all the ingredients for the Marie Rose dip in a small bowl.

Transfer the dip into two small bowls to serve.

Arrange the vegetable sticks into mini buckets, the breadsticks into glasses and the pittas onto a wooden chopping board and hey presto! You have a super-quick and tasty snack.

For the marie rose dip

6 tablespoons mayonnaise

1 tablespoon mango chutney

2 teaspoons Worcestershire sauce

3 teaspoons tomato ketchup

For the crudités

200g carrot, cut into batons

175g baby corn

1 cucumber, cut into chunky sticks

125–150g breadsticks

6 white or wholemeal pittas, toasted and cut into strips

Ham and cheese sliders

MAKES 16

Sliders are simply filled mini rolls with a poppy seed sauce and are very popular with our friends stateside. These sure-fire crowd pleasers take no time at all to prepare and will fill any hungry bellies.

Preheat the oven to 180°C/gas mark 4.

Cut each roll in half horizontally. Spread a generous amount of mayonnaise on one half of each roll and fill with a slice of Cheddar, followed by a slice of ham.

Place the filled sliders into a deep baking tray or casserole dish and set aside.

In a small bowl, mix together the sauce ingredients and pour evenly over the sliders.

Cover with foil and allow the rolls to sit for 10 minutes before baking for 12 minutes or until the cheese is bubbling.

Uncover the rolls and cook for a further 2–3 minutes or until the sliders turn brown and golden on top.

Remove from the oven and immediately place the sliders onto a serving plate.

Stick a toothpick flag into each roll to prevent them from falling apart and serve.

you will need

16 mini white or brown bread rolls
3 tablespoons mayonnaise
16 slices of mild Cheddar
8 slices of honey-roasted ham, halved

for the sauce

120g salted butter, melted
1 tablespoon poppy seeds
1 tablespoon English mustard
1 teaspoon Worcestershire sauce

sos smoothie

Juice or smoothie cartons are perfect for any last-minute party but if you have a few extra minutes, do whip up these delicious and healthy smoothies.

Place the milk and honey into a blender. Break in the bananas and pulse until smooth.

Pour the smoothie into eight 300ml glasses. Serve with a straw and a generous sprinkling of chocolate chips or hundreds and thousands.

you will need

2.25 litres semi-skimmed milk, chilled

8 bananas, peeled

1 heaped tablespoon clear honey

50g chocolate chips or hundreds and thousands

cheesy melting moments

The most moreish savoury treats known to exist, these cheesy delights are a favourite with children – big and small. Kids love getting their hands dirty with the dunking, too, so get them involved in the cooking. Once baked, you will need to serve them immediately.

Preheat the oven to 200°C/gas mark 6. Line two baking trays with baking parchment and set aside.

Place the cream cheese, butter, Cheddar and Parmesan in a saucepan over a low heat until smooth. Set aside.

In a bowl, whisk the egg whites until stiff and then fold into the melted cheese mixture.

Cut the bread into squares – we've found that about 25 squares per slice of bread works well.

Dip each square of bread into the cheese mixture until completely coated and lay on the lined baking trays. (If you like you could freeze them at this point for future use.)

Bake for 10 minutes, turning over once and checking after 5 minutes. The cubes are ready when they are light brown.

Serve piled high in mini buckets or flowerpots.

you will need

75g full-fat cream cheese
150g salted butter
75g mild Cheddar, grated
75g Parmesan cheese, grated
2 large egg whites
6 slices of white bread, crusts removed

Ice cream sundae Bar

SERVES 8

Get the kids to grab a seat, take a bowl and spoon and get started. In this DIY ice cream extravaganza, the guests do the assembly – all you have to do is serve up a ball or two of ice cream and let your little terrors loose with the toppings.

Look like a professional gelato server and ball the ice cream ahead of time. Put the scoops in a large bowl and leave in the freezer until needed.

Make sure you have a varied selection of toppings to keep all your guests happy. In our experience, fresh berries, chopped bananas, smashed Maltesers, chocolate buttons and marshmallows are always popular. Crushed Oreos and gooey choc chip or oaty cookies are delicious with ice cream, too.

you will need

500ml vanilla ice cream

500ml chocolate ice cream

for the toppings

325g chocolate sauce in a squeezy bottle

325g toffee sauce in a squeezy bottle

selection of fresh berries

chopped bananas

Maltesers or smashed chocolate buttons

marshmallows

Crunchie bars, crushed

Oreos cookies, crushed

chocolate chip cookies, crushed

oaty biscuits, crushed

NO-BaKe Sweetie caKe

SERVES 24

You can make this super-quick and easy homemade fridge cake in less time that it would take to get to the supermarket! Just remember that it needs a minimum of 2 hours setting time in the fridge. For a bit of fun, why not place little bowls of the sweets on the party table and allow the children to decorate the birthday cake before lighting the candles and digging in!

Line a 25 x 34cm rectangular baking tin with baking parchment and set aside.

In a medium-sized bowl, use your hands to break up the digestive biscuits into pieces (but not too small). Set aside.

In a medium saucepan, melt the butter, chocolate and syrup over a low heat, stirring occasionally, ensuring the mixture does not burn. Once melted, remove from the heat and leave to cool for 5 minutes.

Once the mixture has cooled, add the crushed biscuits, honeycomb and marshmallows and gently mix together until everything is coated.

Pour the chocolate mixture into the lined tin and immediately transfer to the fridge to set. (Four hours is ideal but you could get away with a minimum of 2 hours. The cake will just have a softer consistency.)

When set, carefully turn the fridge cake onto a chopping board.

Cover the cake with a thin layer of ready-made fudge icing. Finally sprinkle over the sweets, the more random the better.

you will need

300g digestive biscuits

250g unsalted butter

400g dark chocolate (minimum 70 per cent cocoa solids), broken into pieces

3 tablespoons golden syrup

160g honeycomb, crushed

100g mini marshmallows

450g ready-made chocolate fudge icing

150g Smarties or other small coloured chocolates

150g Rolos or chocolate-coated chewy caramels

170g mini fudge chunks

Directory

SPECIALIST SHOPS

Cake Craft World
www.cakecraftworld.co.uk
Great edible and non-edible cake decorations plus cake moulds and tins in every size and shape.

Cakes Cookies & Crafts Shop
www.cakescookiesandcraftsshop.co.uk
This shop has an enormous selection – from pretty party bags to edible glitter in every colour. The cookie cutter collection is fantastic and the website is simple and easy to use.

Cookie Girl
www.cookiegirl.co.uk
Cookie Girl offers cupcake making and decorating classes for all ages. Private lessons are available too.

Jane Asher
www.janeasher.com
A real Aladdin's cave complete with friendly and knowledgeable staff. If you need some baking advice, then a visit to this Chelsea hotspot is a must. They stock everything and anything.

Lakeland
www.lakeland.co.uk
Has a wide range of baking products and is a great place to pick up some presentation props.

Peter Rabbit Organics
www.peterrabbitorganics.co.uk
Delicious organic juices, suitable for 6 months upwards. They come in different flavours and sizes and look pretty on any party table.

Squires
www.squires-shop.com
Squires are based in Farnham, Surrey but they have an impressive online shop too. They also offer classes in basic baking and sugarcraft that will give you confidence in the kitchen.

PARTY SUPPLIES

Amazon
www.amazon.co.uk
However awkward or unlikely your product, chances are Amazon will supply it! Delivery is speedy too.

Carousel Carousel
http://carousel-carousel.com
Carousel is the magic playground of every child's imagination. Stylish decorations, tableware and themed party kits will help you conjure up a sensational event.

Letterbox
www.letterbox.co.uk
Has a huge range of personalised stationery and traditional gifts, plus some cute goodie bag ideas.

Party Delights
www.partydelights.co.uk
Another go to when it comes to tableware, decorations and fancy dress. Or if you are looking for party inspiration in general, then here is a good place to look.

Party Pieces
www.partypieces.co.uk
This company should be on every party planner's speed dial. Well stocked, reliable and convenient, you will find everything you need here, from themed tableware and boxes to party bag fillers and colourful garden lanterns.

HARD TO FIND INGREDIENTS

Candy Melts and Coloured Chocolate
Candy Melts are made by Wilton, which is an American brand but you can buy them in any of the cake supply stores mentioned above and also on Amazon.

Silver Spoon
www.silverspoon.co.uk
Silver Spoon supply flavoured chocolate buttons, which are ideal for cake-pop decorating.

Lavender
There are plenty of places to buy lavender including Amazon, but some other options are:
Lavender Fields
www.thelavenderfields.co.uk
Melbury & Appleton
www.melburyandappleton.co.uk

FOODS FOR ALLERGIES

Doves Farm
www.dovesfarm.co.uk
In our opinion, this is the best place to buy gluten-free baking products. They even offer a gluten-free starter kit.

The Fabulous Bakin' Boys
www.bakinboys.co.uk
If you need some nut-free products, then check these boys

out. All their products are baked in a nut-free factory, so you are safe in the knowledge that any child with a serious allergy will be well looked after.

GoodnessDirect

www.goodnessdirect.co.uk
If you want healthier party food, then pay GoodnessDirect a call. They have a great online range of 'free from' products, from real fruit juice jelly bears to organic smoothie pouches.

MooFree Chocolate

www.moofreechocolates.com
This company has been recommended to us by several clients. They believe MooFree has the best tasting dairy-free chocolate and their children adore it.

The Nut Free Chocolatier

www.thenutfreechocolatier.co.uk
This company sells everything, from fruity chocolate slabs and caramel discs, to marshmallow kebabs and novelty party bag fillers.

Tesco

www.tesco.com
Competitively priced food with a good 'free from' selection. Their mini gluten-free pizzas and cake bars are a great back-up if you are short of time.

Waitrose

www.waitrose.com
Waitrose offer a wide range of 'free from' products that taste good and won't break the bank.

Whole Foods

www.wholefoodsmarket.com
A natural foods supermarket with high-quality products and high standards. Their merchandise is expensive but you really notice a difference in quality and they cater for all allergies and intolerances.

BALLOONS

Circus Circus

www.circuscircus.co.uk
This is a small store in Fulham, London, with an online shop as well. It sells a wide range of fancy dress costumes, themed party tableware and endless balloons.

Non Stop Party Shop

www.nonstopparty.co.uk
There are a total of four Non Stop party shops in the UK and their online store is packed full of products. Not the easiest company to get through to on the phone but once you succeed, staff are helpful and their prices are competitive.

PARTY BAGS

If you are working with a tight budget, then simply visit a large supermarket or joke shop for your party bag fillers. You can put the bags together yourself at home, padding them out with lollipops and fun-sized chocolate bars. However, if you are intending on splashing out on party bags for your guests, then we would suggest that you hit the companies below!

The Little Things

www.lovethelittlethings.co.uk
An online shop that provides a wide range of gift ideas to cover most budgets. They also offer pretty stationery, amusing table decorations and personalised presents.

Star Bags

www.starbags.info
Bespoke, handmade party bags which will cause quite a stir amongst your guests! Beautifully presented treasure, which can even be delivered to your door before your event. If you have money to spend, then Star Bags is a must for you.

MAGAZINES AND WEBSITES

Angels and Urchins

www.angelsandurchins.co.uk
London's indispensable parent's guide. If you can't get your hands on one of the quarterly copies, do not fear, it's all online too.

Baby London

www.babylondon.co.uk
Includes a searchable directory of baby products and services. A good selection of venues and entertainers available for hire are listed here.

The Party Times

www.partypieces.co.uk/thepartytimes/
A thorough, online guide to party planning and home entertaining.

Rascals of London

www.rascalsoflondon.co.uk
If you are after an action packed, out-and-about birthday party, then look at this magazine for inspiration. Endless trip ideas and an up to the minute guide to what's on in your area.

Index

abracadabra pin wheels 62
alien brew 127
allergies 9
apple juice: fizzy orchard squash 57
    scallywags' slushy punch 105
apples: apple nachos 161
    toffee apple cupcakes 139
apricot glaze 17
asteroid belt cookies 119
autumnal leaves 175
avocado: fairy fritters 67

bacon: crispy potato skins 155
    fairy fritters 67
baguettes: baguette boats 100
    rooster's roulade 45
bananas: bears-love-honey shake 37
    cosmic cones 123
    Mungo's monkey shake 147
    SOS smoothie 197
bears-love-honey shake 37
beef: shooting burger planets 114
beetroot: autumnal leaves 175
biscuits: asteroid belt cookies 119
    carnival stick cookies 136
    cheesy farmyard friends 46
    Elly elephants 140
    explosive mars meteors 120–2
    gingerbread ted 29
    land of milk and honey 90
    marshmallow sheep biscuits 53
    no-bake sweetie cake 202–3
    pirate Jack gingersnaps 102
    strawberry biscuit towers 83
blackberries: fizzy orchard squash 57
blackcurrant: HMS jellies 109
blueberries: drop scone horseshoes 158
    fresh fruity wands with popping candy 68
    jam pot jelly jars 30
bread: baguette boats 100
    cheesy melting moments 199
    fairy bread 64
    ham and cheese sliders 196
    Monsieur Teddy 25
    rooster's roulade 45
    shooting burger planets 114
    tear and share bread 152
    wizard's cheesy cauldron 66
brownies, hobgoblin's gooey 70
burgers: shooting burger planets 114
butter icing 17
buttermilk: farmers' muffins 49
    Martians' fingers 118
butterscotch: apple nachos 161

cakes 10
    chocolate sponge 16
    clown cake 144–6
    fairy dust cupcakes 72
    farmyard cake 54–6
    glittery gem cake pops 84
    hobgoblin's gooey brownies 70
    knight and princess castle cake 86–8
    no-bake sweetie cake 202–3
    rocket cake 124–6
    sheriff's badge cake 164–6
    spooktacular ghost cake 184–6
    teddy bear cake 34–6
    toffee apple cupcakes 139
    treasure map cake 106–8
    white chocolate vanilla sponge 16
caramel: toffee apple cupcakes 139
carnival stick cookies 136
carrots: veggie dip pots 195
cheese: abracadabra pin wheels 62
    baguette boats 100
    cheesy farmyard friends 46
    cheesy melting moments 199
    crispy potato skins 155
    DIY pizzas 192
    farmers' muffins 49
    floundering fish cones 96
    ham and cheese sliders 196
    juggler's popcorn bowls 135
    Monsieur Teddy 25
    naan ghost pizzas 183
    palace pancetta pies 78
    ringmaster's nacho cups 143
    shooting burger planets 114
    sizzling fajitas with easy peasy salsa 156
    tear and share bread 152
    vegetable sea dome 99
    wizard's cheesy cauldron 66
    see also cream cheese; mascarpone
cherries: Mama's cherry pies 163
chicken: chicken porky pies 42
    Martians' fingers 118
    sizzling fajitas with easy peasy salsa 156
chickpeas: Dracula's stew 176
chocolate: apple nachos 161
    chocolate birds' nests 50
    chocolate butter icing 17
    chocolate fudge icing 17
    chocolate pumpkins 180
    chocolate sponge 16
    clown cake 144–6
    cosmic cones 123
    Elly elephants 140

explosive mars meteors 120–2
farmyard cake 54–6
glittery gem cake pops 84
hobgoblin's gooey brownies 70
ice cream sundae bar 200
knight and princess castle cake 86–8
marshmallow sheep biscuits 53
no-bake sweetie cake 202–3
pixie's potion 65
ready teddy goo goo 26
rocket cake 124–6
royal fruit buckets 89
sheriff's badge cake 164–6
SOS smoothie 197
spooktacular ghost cake 184–6
teddy bear cake 34–6
treasure map cake 106–8
vampire pots 179
white chocolate vanilla sponge 16
chorizo: naan ghost pizzas 183
    ringmaster's nacho cups 143
circus, circus 128–47
clown cake 144–6
cod: floundering fish cones 96
cola: alien brew 127
cookies: asteroid belt cookies 119
    carnival stick cookies 136
    land of milk and honey 90
    pirate Jack gingersnaps 102
cornflakes: chocolate birds' nests 50
    Martians' fingers 118
cosmic cones 123
courgettes: farmers' muffins 49
craft activities 40, 60, 76, 94
cream: mermaid shell meringues 101
    strawberry biscuit towers 83
cream cheese: cheesy melting moments 199
    fairy fritters 67
    knights' and ladies' shield puffs 80
    rooster's roulade 45
    tear and share bread 152
    ted's pea pots 22
crisps: autumnal leaves 175
crispy potato skins 155
cucumber: rooster's roulade 45
    vegetable sea dome 99
    veggie dip pots 195
cupcakes: fairy dust 72
    toffee apple cupcakes 139
custard: jam pot jelly jars 30

dips: ted's pea pots 22
    veggie dip pots 195
DIY pizzas 192

Dracula's stew 176
dressing, ranch 157
drinks: alien brew 127
    bears-love-honey shake 37
    fizzy orchard squash 57
    the gunslinger 167
    land of milk and honey 90
    pixie's potion 65
    scallywags' slushy punch 105
    slimy lime grime 187
    SOS smoothie 197
drop scone horseshoes 158
dulce de leche: toffee apple cupcakes 139

eggs: chocolate pumpkins 180
    mermaid shell meringues 101
    palace pancetta pies 78
    vampire pots 179
    veiny devilled eggs 172
Elly elephants 140
entertainers 13–14, 40, 61, 76, 130, 170
explosive mars meteors 120–2

fairies and wizards 58–73
fairy bread 64
fairy dust cupcakes 72
fairy fritters 67
fajitas with easy peasy salsa 156
fancy dress 11, 13, 60, 150, 170
farmers' muffins 49
farmyard cake 54–6
farmyard fun 38–57
finger lickin' ribs 157
fish: floundering fish cones 96
    knights' and ladies' shield puffs 80
fizzy orchard squash 57
floundering fish cones 96
food presentation 10–11, 20, 76, 151
fritters, fairy 67
frosting, mascarpone 139
fruit: fresh fruity wands with popping candy 68
    royal fruit buckets 89
    see also individual types of fruit
fudge: chocolate fudge icing 17
    no-bake sweetie cake 202–3

games 13, 20, 40, 61, 94–5, 113, 130, 150–1, 171, 190
gammon: baguette boats 100
ghosts, ghouls and goblins 168–87
ginger: gingerbread ted 29
    the gunslinger 167
    pirate Jack gingersnaps 102
    scallywags' slushy punch 105

glaze, apricot 17
glittery gem cake pops 84
'going home' presents 20, 40, 61, 76, 95, 113, 130, 151, 171, 190
golden wedges 81
goo goo cakes 26
grapes: fresh fruity wands with popping candy 68
    royal fruit buckets 89
the gunslinger 167

ham: abracadabra pin wheels 62
    baguette boats 100
    DIY pizzas 192
    ham and cheese sliders 196
    rooster's roulade 45
    helter skelter sausages 132
    HMS jellies 109
    hobgoblin's gooey brownies 70
honeycomb: bears-love-honey shake 37
    explosive mars meteors 120-2
    no-bake sweetie cake 202-3

ice cream: alien brew 127
    ice cream sundae bar 200
icings 17
    butter 17
    chocolate fudge 17
    mascarpone frosting 139
intolerances 9
invitations 8-9

jam pot jelly jars 30
jelly: HMS jellies 109
    jam pot jelly jars 30
juggler's popcorn bowls 135

kiwi: fresh fruity wands with popping candy 68
knights and princesses 74-91

land of milk and honey 90
last-minute panic party 188-203
lavender: Elly elephants 140
    land of milk and honey 90
lemonade: slimy lime grime 187
    scallywags' slushy punch 105
lettuce: rooster's roulade 45
limes: HMS jellies 109
    slimy lime grime 187

Mama's cherry pies 163
marie rose dip 195
marshmallows: apple nachos 161
    cosmic cones 123
    explosive mars meteors 120-2
    marshmallow sheep biscuits 53
    no-bake sweetie cake 202-3
    ready teddy goo goo 26
Martians' fingers 118
mascarpone: Mama cherry pies 163
    toffee apple cupcakes 139
menu choices 9-10, 20, 190
meringues, mermaid shell 101

milk: bears-love-honey shake 37
    land of milk and honey 90
    Mungo's monkey shake 147
    pixie's potion 65
    SOS smoothie 197
mini Sputnik spuds 117
Monsieur Teddy 25
muffins, farmers' 49
Mungo's monkey shake 147
mushrooms: DIY pizzas 192

naan ghost pizzas 183
nachos: apple 161
    ringmaster's nacho cups 143
no-bake sweetie cake 202-3

olives: chicken porky pies 42
    DIY pizzas 192
    naan ghost pizzas 183
onions: Dracula's stew 176
    sizzling fajitas with easy peasy salsa 156
oranges: chocolate pumpkins 180
    the gunslinger 167
    HMS jellies 109
orchard squash, fizzy 57

palace pancetta pies 78
pancetta: farmers' muffins 49
    mini Sputnik spuds 117
    palace pancetta pies 78
    tear and share bread 152
    wizard's cheesy cauldron 66
parsnips: autumnal leaves 175
party bags 20, 40, 61, 76, 95, 113, 130, 151, 171, 190
passion fruit: strawberry biscuit towers 83
pastry: abracadabra pin wheels 62
    chicken porky pies 42
    helter skelter sausages 132
    knights' and ladies' shield puffs 80
    Mama's cherry pies 163
    turkey in blankets 33
peas: easy peasy salsa 156
    knights' and ladies' shield puffs 80
    ted's pea pots 22
pepperoni: DIY pizzas 192
peppers: DIY pizzas 192
    sizzling fajitas with easy peasy salsa 156
pesto: baguette boats 100
    Monsieur Teddy 25
    naan ghost pizzas 183
pies: chicken porky pies 42
    Mama's cherry pies 163
pineapple: fresh fruity wands with popping candy 68
    scallywags' slushy punch 105
pirate Jack gingersnaps 102
pittas: veggie dip pots 195
pixie's potion 65
pizza: DIY pizzas 192

naan ghost pizzas 183
popcorn: juggler's popcorn bowls 135
popping candy: explosive mars meteors 120-2
    fresh fruity wands with popping candy 68
poppy seeds: golden wedges 81
    ham and cheese sliders 196
pork: finger lickin' ribs 157
potatoes: autumnal leaves 175
    crispy potato skins 155
    golden wedges 81
    mini Sputnik spuds 117
pretzels: Martians' fingers 118
princesses and knights 74-91
prizes 13
punch, scallywags' slushy 105

ranch dressing 157
raspberries: jam pot jelly jars 30
ready teddy goo goo 26
Rice Krispies: ready teddy goo goo 26
ringmaster's nacho cups 143
rocket cake 124-6
rooster's roulade 45
royal fruit buckets 89

salmon: knights' and ladies' shield puffs 80
salsa, easy peasy 156
sandwiches: baguette boats 100
    ham and cheese sliders 196
    Monsieur Teddy 25
    rooster's roulade 45
sausages: Dracula's stew 176
    helter skelter sausages 132
    ringmaster's nacho cups 143
scallywags' slushy punch 105
sheep biscuits, marshmallow 53
sheriff's badge cake 164-6
shooting burger planets 114
sizzling fajitas with easy peasy salsa 156
slimy lime grime 187
smoothies: Mungo's monkey shake 147
    SOS smoothie 197
space and star odyssey 110-27
spare ribs, finger lickin' 157
spinach: wizard's cheesy cauldron 66
sponge fingers: vampire pots 179
spooktacular ghost cake 184
squash, fizzy orchard 57
stew, Dracula's 176
strawberries: fresh fruity wands with popping candy 68
    HMS jellies 109
    royal fruit buckets 89
    strawberry biscuit towers 83
sweet potatoes: autumnal leaves 175
    golden wedges 81
sweetcorn: chicken porky pies 42
    fairy fritters 67

ringmaster's nacho cups 143
veggie dip pots 195

tarts: palace pancetta pies 78
tear and share bread 152
teddy bear cake 34-6
teddy bears' picnic 18-37
ted's pea pots 22
thank you notes 14
themes 6
toffee: apple nachos 161
    ice cream sundae bar 200
    ready teddy goo goo 26
    toffee apple cupcakes 139
tomatoes: baguette boats 100
    DIY pizzas 192
    Dracula's stew 176
    naan ghost pizzas 183
    ringmaster's nacho cups 143
    rooster's roulade 45
    shooting burger planets 114
    sizzling fajitas with easy peasy salsa 156
    turkey in blankets 33
    vegetable sea dome 99
    wizard's cheesy cauldron 66
tortillas: sizzling fajitas with easy peasy salsa 156
treasure map cake 106-8
turkey in blankets 33

under the sea 92-109

vampire pots 179
vanilla: pixie's potion 65
    white chocolate vanilla sponge 16
vegetables: autumnal leaves 175
    vegetable sea dome 99
    veggie dip pots 195
    see also individual types of vegetable
veiny devilled eggs 176
venues 6, 8

watermelon: vegetable sea dome 99
wild, wild west 148-67
wizards and fairies 58-73
wizard's cheesy cauldron 66

yogurt: finger lickin' ribs 157

Thank yous

We would like to say a huge thank you to everyone who has helped bring Hats & Bells to life!

To Kyle Cathie, Judith Hannam and Vicky Orchard at Kyle Books. Thank you for taking a chance on us and our first book.

It would not have been possible without our fabulous production team: Jemma Watts, whose photographs helped bring our ideas to reality; Pippa Jameson, whose style and attention to detail perfectly mirrored our vision; Gee Charman, for making our recipes look so lovely and Lucy Parissi, for her gorgeous design.

To our irreplaceable 'Fairy Godmother' Heather Holden-Brown at HHB Agency and her girls, Claire Houghton-Price and Elly James.

Clare Hulton, who believed in our idea.

Our models who were fantastic and patient: Alfie Brigstocke, Emily Brigstocke, Arthur Fortescue, Aliyah Goodwin, Amaan Goodwin, Poppy Lawson Johnston, Jessica Popoola, Summer Showell, Lorenzo Stock, Charlie Thomas, Oliver Thomas, Aimee White, Gemma White, Lucy White, Archie Wolseley Brinton, Fred Wolseley Brinton and William Wolseley Brinton.

We would also like to thank the following suppliers: VV Rouleaux; BHS; Paula Beades; Argos and dotcomgiftshop.com.

Annabel's Thank Yous

To all the Waley-Cohens, in particular Felicity and those exuberant jelly-making sessions! Linda, you were a star for letting us run riot in your kitchen.

My wonderful parents, Bertie and Serena, and siblings, Ed and Chloe. Thank you all for supporting me when I 'jumped ship' from acting to party planning. You were hugely positive about my new venture and I have loved brainstorming and experimenting with you over the years. Your constant love, encouragement and invaluable guidance is what spurs me on. I look forward to many more 'culinary experiences' with you all, both at home and in the south of France!

Finally, to my boys. My heavenly new baby Maximilian and my darling husband Sam. You are an inspiration. Every year you raise your game to unfathomable heights. Whether it's on the back of a racehorse, at work or quietly dreaming with me at home, somehow you surmount the insurmountable. Here's to years of laughter, love and.....children's parties!

Hatty's Thank Yous

First and foremost, I would like to thank my parents whose unfaltering love and support has always given me strength and courage to pursue my dreams. You both mean the world to me.

My sisters, Emily and Annabelle, and my brother David, who have always been there to smooth out the bumps in the road. I am so proud of you all and forever grateful for all the love and advice.

Gareth, who has been a wise sounding board throughout and who reliably remains calm and encouraging when I'm going through my most testing days. Thank you for your love and never-ending support.

Lastly, my housemate and amazing friend Libby, for being incredibly patient, a great tester and for always being on hand with a glass of wine at the end of an exhausting day. Thank you.